Broken Shore

Books by Arthur Quinn

The Confidence of British Philosophers
Broken Shore: The Marin Peninsula — A Perspective on History
Figures of Speech
Before Abraham Was

Broken Shore

The Marin Peninsula In California History

Arthur Quinn

REDWOOD PRESS
INVERNESS, CALIFORNIA

Originally published as *Broken Shore: The Marin Peninsula — A Perspective on History*
© 1981 by Peregrine Smith, Inc.
All Rights Reserved

This paperback edition published by special arrangement with Arthur Quinn

REDWOOD PRESS
Post Office Box 776
Inverness, California 94937
415-663-8384

First Printing 1987 5 4 3 2 1
Printed and bound in the United States of America

Cover, map, and index © by Redwood Press
Cover design by Wendy Schwartz based on a nineteenth century lithograph by Britton, Rey & Company, S.F.
Map by Dewey Livingston
Printed on acid-free paper by McNaughton & Gunn, Inc.

Library of Congress Cataloging in Publication Data

Quinn, Arthur.
    Broken shore.

    Bibliography: p.
    Includes index.
    1. Marin Peninsula (Calif.) — History. I. Title.
F868.M3Q56 1987 979.4'62 86-20362

ISBN 0-939061-00-7 (pbk.:alk. paper)

Contents

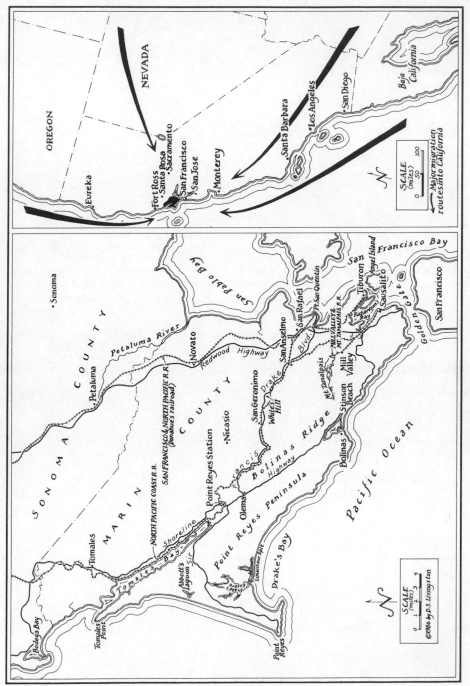

The Marin Peninsula and California

                              It
     is certain the world cannot be stopped nor saved.
It has changes to accomplish and must creep through agonies
        toward a new discovery. It must, and it ought: the awful
        necessity
Is also the sacrificial duty. Man's world is a tragic music and is not
        played for man's happiness,
Its discords are not resolved but by other discords.

                    Robinson Jeffers, "Going to Horse Flats"

Better to carve suns and moons on the joints of crosses
as was done in my district. To birches and firs
give feminine names. To implore protection
against the mute and treacherous might
than to proclaim, as you did, an inhuman thing.

                    Czeslaw Milosz, "To Robinson Jeffers"

Broken Shore

History first waded onto the Marin Peninsula in
1579 as an able pirate on a run of good luck . . .

The Coyote's Head and the Sierra Nevada
Courtesy of NASA

Prologue

The broken shore now called the Marin Peninsula is really two peninsulas, strangely juxtaposed, as if at cross-purposes. The main peninsula, to which the other seems to some a mere appendage, is the Marin Peninsula proper. It stretches from north to south, toward other land which it almost touches (but nowhere does), thereby helping form a large bay still mothered by the sea. Into this bay, Marin sends a series of sub-peninsulas, creating coves of shelter, with a few islands punctuating these. But on the sea side of Marin is the different story; there, attached to Marin but not simply part of it, is the rival peninsula, Point Reyes, stretching east to west, out into the open sea.

Point Reyes and Marin are not merely contrary in their orientation, one to land, the other to sea; they differ in their very substance. The foundation of Point Reyes was laid in granite—grey granite, speckled black on white, crystalline, solid as a rock should be, refined deep inside the earth, risen somehow in its purity to the surface, a thing from which monuments more lasting than human memory can be wrought. The larger Marin Peninsula has its foundation in less exalted stuff, matter in fact so common, so heterogeneous, its manner of coming to be is a deep puzzlement.

Franciscan Formation is the name attached to this perplexing mixture of rocks on which the Marin Peninsula is founded. A "nightmare of rocks" one guidebook called it, a nightmare for anyone who wishes to comprehend it. And within this nightmare there is one rock characteristic of the enigma. A greenish rock, sometimes a mottled blackish-green like the bay on a clouded day, it is a kind of soapstone, a little slimy to the touch. This greenish, slightly slimy rock is aptly named serpentine, the serpent rock. Moreover, it bears with it, like its rattles, the most arresting minerals of the whole

3

Franciscan Formation, minerals for which there is no equivalent in the austere purity of Point Reyes: the lucent, aqueous crystals of the bluecrist; the fire red powder of cinnabar; the complex green of jade, in appearance at once solid and liquid; and even the rare manganese ores, colored like the moods of a geologist confronted with the nightmare of the Franciscan, usually a blank black, occasionally a deeply shocked pink.

Serpentine and granite, land and sea, there is still another contrast between these two strangely juxtaposed peninsulas—their shapes. The Marin Peninsula lacks, in a sense, any shape at all. It reaches to the south, and to the east fingers the bay it helped create; but all this it does without detectable regularity. Its shape is the shape of itself, and nothing else. It fails to tell the human eye of other things.

Point Reyes, in contrast, risks losing itself in the telling. At its north a loch separates much of Point Reyes from Marin, until it finally ends at the land which bridges the two. Parallel to this loch, at its entrance on Point Reyes' side, is an elegantly tapered point called Tomales. Tomales provides the key to the seaward peninsula's complete figure. Tomales is shaped like an ear, the pointed, alert ear of a wild dog, perhaps of the coyote, which once was so abundant here. And, as the beach curves from Point Tomales to the west toward Point Reyes itself, it does straighten as a forehead should, and where the eye should be is a large lagoon. And the blunted granite of Point Reyes does suggest a snout. And the coastline as it moves south from Point Reyes does curve gently as would a throat, and just before that curve there is a gaping estuary for a mouth. And who, having seen all this, would not notice that below the throat, just before being absorbed back into the mainland of Marin, the land does bulge a bit, into the sea, as if to hint a chest?

Of course, if one looks too closely, he sees nothing at all, or rather all that is wrong. The ear is a bit too long, the snout too broad; the lagoon would make a misshapen eye, the estuary a monstrous mouth. Yet if one does not look too closely, things will be plain enough. Behind the Marin Peninsula, to the human eye shapeless and ill-founded, will rise Point Reyes—the coyote head, alert, breathing, listening, and facing out onto the open sea.

I
Nova Albion

History first waded onto the Marin Peninsula in 1579 as an able pirate on a run of good luck.

Francis Drake did annex the Marin Peninsula and the surrounding territory in the name of his virgin Queen, England's Elizabeth, and posted a brass plaque as a token. His expedition was, nonetheless, not one of exploration or possession, but rather of simple theft. He and his band of men had entered the Pacific Ocean in order to commit acts of piracy against Spanish shipping and settlements.

Not that the crew seems to have known that they were signing on for such a voyage. Drake apparently had not been entirely candid with them, and many thought they were agreeing to a more orthodox type of international trade, a voyage which would present dangers enough for a brave man. But when Drake turned his three ships toward the Pacific, it was clear that he intended his men to face not just the sea, but the dangers of being an outlaw as well.

Before the ships had even reached the Pacific, Drake was himself faced with an incipient mutiny. Now the time had come to educate his men in his ways, to make their fear of faceless Spaniards fade before their fear of Francis Drake. He forced the crew to bring to trial the most prominent of his critics, a man who actually had command of one of his ships. To the crew as jury, Drake, both prosecutor and judge, presented his summation.

"My masters, you may say whether this fellow hath sought my discredit or no, and what should be meant hereby but the very overthrow of the voyage: first by taking away my good name, and altogether discrediting me; and then by taking my life. Which if I am bereaved of, what then will you do? If you think you will be able to drink another's blood, and so be able to return again unto your own

5

country, you will never be able to find the way there. And now, my masters, consider what a great voyage we are likely to make, the like of which was never made out of England. And by this same voyage the worst in this fleet shall become a gentleman. But if this voyage go not forward—which I cannot see how possible it should if this man live—what a reproach it will be not only unto our country but especially unto us? Even the simplest here may consider this. Therefore, my masters, they that think this man worthy to die let them with me hold up their hands, and they that think him not worthy to die hold down their hands."

The vote of my masters was in favor of Drake, his name, his life, a successful voyage, a safe return home, fame, wealth, position, honor, country, and the death of a man. Two days after the trial, John Doughty (that was his name) was beheaded. And scarcely had his head fallen from his trunk than Francis Drake was triumphantly thrusting it aloft, shouting at the crew, "Loo, this is the end of traitors!" And, loo, for the rest of the voyage, there were no more traitors among my masters.

By the time Drake and his men had reached the Marin Peninsula, the memory of Doughty's execution must have almost faded into a natural passing, so much had happened in between. Soon after entering the Pacific, Drake had lost two of his three ships. Then his luck had changed, as he had expected it would. His single ship ravished Spanish shipping, so that by the time he entered California waters its ballast was silver and gold. Drake was well on his way to becoming Sir Francis. All he needed to do was to find his way back home.

But finding a way home proved no simple matter. Drake had entered California waters possibly in the hope of finding the fabled strait of Anian, which was said to connect the northern Pacific with the northern Atlantic. He had had so much good fortune, why not the honor of such a discovery as well? Here he had pressed his luck. He had gone far to the north, into completely uncharted waters beyond California, only to be forced to turn back in the end. His ship was leaking, his men exhausted, his stores low. He sought a port where the ship could be careened and repaired, the men rested, the stores replenished.

The Elizabethan mariner was a man unusually superstitious even in a superstitious age. He had committed his life to the sea, that least reliable element of his world. And he had done so in ships that could barely protect him in the best of times. So much at the sea's mercy, the mariner could not but believe he could see, if dimly, reasons behind its caprices.

Drake, the Elizabethan captain, knew the superstitious disposition of his crew to be one of his resources of command. He might share some of these superstitions, but he could not afford to indulge himself. He knew his crew to be almost as unruly an element as the sea. As he established a fear of himself, so he used their fear of the sea, that fear which had been ritualized as superstition, to his own ends.

Among the charges Drake had raised against John Doughty was the conjuring up of bad winds—no expedition could survive with a malevolent magus on board. Drake could use superstition to create fear, or to calm it. Before entering the Pacific, he had made great show of changing the name of his flagship from the mundane *Pelican* to the mythical *Golden Hind*—such a name had to bring good luck to any vessel that took it.

So, Drake would have had little difficulty explaining to his crew what it meant when in the midst of their search for a haven they found what looked to be the white cliffs of Dover. What surer sign that this was meant to be their harbor? Not only were the cliffs English, so was the weather, nipping cold and drizzly fog.

Francis Drake and his *Golden Hind* sought safe harbor somewhere near the white cliffs that constitute the western-most extension of the Marin Peninsula, most likely in the bay which is sheltered by these cliffs of Point Reyes. Drake claimed this harbor and the land surrounding it to be a new England, "Nova Albion."

Now Drake had to worry that his luck would hold. Careening and repairing the ship would take the better part of a month, during which time he would be more vulnerable to attack than he ever was at sea. He did not have to worry much about Spanish patrols this far north, but he had to worry about the local natives.

They did appear to be friendly. A local chief had, whether he knew it or not, actually participated in the ceremony which formally annexed his land to the English crown. Nonetheless, Drake had already experienced how treacherous such natives could be. In South America Drake and a landing party had been nearly massacred by an apparently friendly group of natives. Drake had lost three men, and himself had escaped only with a serious arrow wound to his face which could easily have cost him an eye. In Nova Albion, however English its appearance, Drake would remain on his guard; he would also do his best to see that his men did not provoke the natives. That meant his crew had to stay away from the women.

The chaplain who wrote the chief account of Drake's stay in Nova Albion presents the crew as pious folk concerned about the immortal souls of the Indians. Chaplain Fletcher assures his readers that when the men observed the native religious services "we groaned in spirit to see the power of Satan so far prevail in seducing these so harmless soules." Even the natives' friendly interest in Drake and his men gave the chaplain a bit of theological unease. "They drew near, as men ravished in their minds with the sight of such things as they never had seen, or heard of before that time: their errand being rather with submission and fear to worship us as Gods."

Drake saw things from a somewhat different perspective. He knew his crew. They might be passionately religious to the man when faced with the immediate dangers of the sea; however, once safely back on shore, they behaved quite differently. And now, after a long and difficult time at sea, chance had placed them in the midst of natives who seemed to defer to them as Gods. The men might think this wholly good luck; Drake did not.

To make matters even worse, the women were scantily clad. To cover their upper body, they had only a deer skin draped about their shoulders; and to cover what the chaplain discreetly called "that which nature teaches should be hidden" they had only a loosely fitting skirt of tules. The chaplain could, if he was so inclined, indulge in the luxury of worrying about seductions of the Devil and ravishings of the mind; Francis Drake had to worry about seductions and ravishings that could have more immediately disagreeable consequences.

Despite the barrier of language, Drake did his best to communicate his concern to the Indians themselves. They must have their women conduct themselves more carefully about his men, no matter how godly they looked. First he tried to demonstrate to them that "we were no gods" (a proposition any Spaniard would have taken as self-evident). Drake had the natives present while he ate and drank with demonstrative relish. Would they not realize that if we shared with them the need for food and drink, we also had certain other bodily needs in common with them? Needs which in the present circumstances could only be satisfied at their expense? No, they seemed incapable of drawing that inference. As Fletcher put it, "Nothing could persuade them, nor remove that opinion, which they had conceived of us."

That was not all they were going to "conceive of us" if Drake could not somehow communicate with them. He tried another approach, this time using clothes. The fact that Drake's men wore clothes should show that they were but men and had "need of such things to cover our own shame." Even if the natives did not perceive the connection between clothes and lust, Drake thought he could at least succeed with them indirectly. Perhaps he could convince them to imitate their new gods. So Drake gave to "each of them liberally, good and necessary things to cover their nakedness." Drake, however, did not understand the natives' customs. His liberal gifts had caught them unprepared. They would be impolite if they did not give ample gifts in return. So they began to give to Drake and his men whatever items of worth they had at hand. They gave them the feathers from their hair, quivers of arrows; and finally they began to give Drake's men the very clothes which "their women wore upon their bodies." What had begun as a calculated lesson in modesty had ended with an innocent strip-tease.

At this point Drake must have realized he was at the mercy of his fates. One can imagine the threats Drake made against anyone caught with a native woman. The image of Doughty's bloody head must have been conjured up more than once. But any such verbal magic was being continually and unknowingly undone by the Indians themselves.

The helplessness to which the ordinarily resourceful Drake had been reduced was demonstrated during one of the lengthy orations the native leaders periodically addressed to the English. Out of courtesy, Drake would have his men attend to words they did not comprehend. Presumably, the natives thought the new gods could understand their language, although they did not deign to speak it. During one of these orations, the women suddenly went into a frenzy, as Fletcher records.

"The women, as if they had been desperate, used unnatural violence against themselves, crying and shrieking piteously, tearing their flesh with their nails from their cheeks, in a monstrous manner, the blood streaming down along their breasts; besides despoiling the upper parts of their bodies of those single coverings they formerly had, and holding their hands above their heads, that they might not rescue their breasts from harm, they would with fury cast themselves upon the ground, never respecting whether it be clean or soft, but dashed themselves in this manner on hard stones, knobby hillocks, stocks of wood, and pricking bushes, or whatever else lay in their way, iterating the same course again and again."

What was Drake to do with his gaping men? Have them go physically restrain these women from continuing to throw their now naked bodies on pricking bushes? He did what was the only thing left. He ordered his men to raise their hands and their eyes to heaven, in prayer.

Somehow Drake's prayers, and not those of his men, were answered. Somehow he managed to spend the weeks in Nova Albion without serious incident over a woman. Drake himself could not have quite understood how it had managed to work out so well. Perhaps the memory of Doughty's blood had a stronger hold than he thought.

A somewhat different answer is suggested by the record Drake's expedition brought back of the native language. There had been worked out a meager list of vocabulary words in the native tongue of Nova Albion. This list, with suggested English meanings, was published with the accounts of the voyage. Twentieth century anthropologists have checked the list and the suggested meanings against what is now known of the native tongue of the Marin Peninsula. They have found the correspondences to be remarkably good. There are no important discrepancies, except one.

This occurs on a word list that seems to have had its origin independent of that kept by the chaplain. The phrase in question is recorded as "nocharo mu." This is relatively close to the common Marin native phrase, "nochato mu." It is the meanings that are askew. Anthropologists say that "nochato mu" means "on the other side." Drake's crew thought "nocharo mu" meant "touch me not." An episode which could have given rise to this strange misunderstanding is not hard to imagine.

A crewman slips away from his fellows, and finds a native woman alone. The risk does not seem great, and he decides to try his luck. He starts to make advances, and she seems willing enough. But then, at the last moment, a cultural difference intrudes.

She gently pushes him away, turns her back, and says quietly, "Nochato mu." "Nocharo mu?" he repeats to himself. Well, he has had women before who liked to play coy at the end. He grabs her and tries to turn her around. But she only shoves him away and says more firmly, "Nochato mu." Now he is puzzled about what has gone wrong, and hesitates. She is becoming impatient, and now says again, somewhat louder, "Nochato mu." He at this point is backing away; and when she starts to raise her voice—"Nocha..."—he turns and runs.

He returns to the ship, disappointed but able to share with his mates an important discovery—these Indian women are just flirts. She returns to her village, also disappointed but able to share with her confidantes an important discovery—these gods from the sea are no men. And Francis Drake, without ever knowing it, has once again been blest by his star.

That the first Europeans who landed on the Marin peninsula were themselves plunderers riding a mythical beast, a golden hind, itself loaded with precious metal—that the landing in outline appears to be a thing of romance—is appropriate. The whole of the early European approach to California had been perceived through the marvellous perspective of romance.

In the sixteenth century many marvels had been projected onto the unexplored reaches of North America by European fancy. Somewhere on that continent, or near its shores, were known to exist but yet to be found: islands with pearls as plentiful as pebbles, lakes with bottoms of gold, fountains of youth, a city of turquoise, and a single diamond so large it could easily be mistakened for an ice-capped peak. Such unprecedented places obviously had to be inhabited by unprecedented peoples. One group lived entirely underwater; members of another boasted of elephantine ears which could clothe them in winter and shade them in summer; a third needed no food, but could grow fat on mere smells. As one recounter of such tales reasoned, "For anyone who will consider the marvels which God constantly does perform in the world, it will be easy to believe that since He is able to create these He may have done so."

In a world where nothing humanly imaginable is beyond Divine omnipotence, and where that omnipotence so often chooses to defy the specifically human sense of decorum—in a world where grizzly bears feed, redwood trees grow, and granite mountains shudder, the line between romance and reality must itself often seem to be the only thing that is certainly pure romance.

And in such a world it should not be surprising that the supposedly fictitious should somehow become real, that a place invented only for the sake of romance should be searched after by real men in real ships. Such was the isle of California, the existence of which was first imagined in 1510 in Garcia Ordones de Montalvo's epic romance, *The Exploits of Esplandian.*

Among Esplandian's many fabulous exploits in defense of Christendom was his double conquest of an Amazon queen, first by his comely appearance, later by his flawless sword play. She was vanquished, his to do with as he wished; and he, somewhat ungraciously, consigned her to the marriage bed of one of his followers. This queen who had traveled so far to try her prowess with Christian knights was named Calafia, and her island kingdom was called California.

The queen of California, if we are to believe Montalvo, was extraordinarily beautiful. Perhaps Esplandian was able to resist her ample charms because he was as distracted as Montalvo by the beast she routinely rode, a beast that was without exaggeration "the strangest that ever was seen."

"It had ears as large as two shields; a broad forehead which had but one eye, like a mirror; the openings of its nostrils were very large but its nose was short and blunt. From its mouth turned up two tusks, each of them two palms long. Its color was yellow, and it had many violet spots upon its skin, like an ounce."

Perhaps Esplandian could not take his eyes off this monstrosity. But perhaps also he had received some reliable intelligence about the fatal charm of Calafia's island home. It was certainly the kind of place a Montalvo would only wish to write about, and not to visit.

"Know, then, that on the right hand of the Indies, there is an island called California, very close to the side of Terrestial Paradise, and it was peopled by black women, without any man among them, for they lived in the fashion of Amazons. They were of strong and hardy bodies, of ardent courage and great force. Their island was the strongest in all the world, with its steep cliffs and rocky shores. Their arms were all of gold, and so was the harness of the wild beasts which they tamed and rode. For, in the whole island, there was no metal but gold. They lived in caves wrought out of the rock with much labor. They had many ships with which they sailed out to obtain booty."

An impregnable island fortress riddled with gold—there was

certainly nothing about this to discourage a knight, unless perhaps he thought a cave an unsuitable abode for noble blood. However, Montalvo had saved the least attractive feature of California to the last.

"In this island, called California, there were many griffins, on account of the great ruggedness of the country, and its infinite host of wild beasts, such as never were seen in any other part of the world. And when the griffins were yet small, the women went out with traps to take them. They covered themselves over with very thick hides, and when they had caught the little griffins they took them to their caves, and brought them up there. And being themselves quite a match for the griffins, they fed them with the men whom they took prisoners, and with the boys to whom they gave birth, and brought them up with such arts that they got much good from them, and no harm. Every man who landed on the island was immediately devoured by these griffins; and although they had had their fill, nonetheless the gorged griffins would seize the remaining men, and carry them high up in the air in their flight; and when they were tired of carrying them, they would let them fall anywhere, to their death."

The Exploits of Esplandian was a rousing success among male Spanish readers of the sixteenth century. In fact, Cervantes tells us it was an important ingredient in the belated education of Don Quixote; indeed, it was the very first book chosen by Quixote's priest for the bonfire by which he hoped—falsely, it turned out—to bring the old gallant back to his senses.

And the Knight of the Doleful Countenance was not the only fabled Spaniard of the period whose life, for better or worse, was influenced by this book. Another cut an even more dashing figure. He was the real conquistador of the Aztecs, Hernan Cortes.

Shortly after his epic exploits against the Aztecs, Cortes began to look toward the north for new pagan civilizations to plunder for his God and his Emperor. However, his Emperor, unlike his God, had to approve. Cortes was in no position to conquer him by force, so he had to resort to the unseemly instrument of persuasion.

In 1524, in the fourth of his famous five letters from Mexico, Cortes passed along to Charles V a reliable piece of intelligence. There was said to be to the northwest of Mexico, on the way to the East Indies, an island kingdom peopled by Amazons; the island itself was said to be rich in gold and pearls.

Although Cortes had wisely substituted the pearls for the griffins, Charles V does not seem to have been entirely convinced. Perhaps he had read the same romance. The first ships Cortes had built for the expedition against the island kingdom were instead sent by the Emperor directly to the East Indies, whose fabled riches had been more authoritatively documented.

It was not until 1535 that Cortes was finally able to send two ships north. By this time the star of Cortes was on the descent. Cortes even had a rival to his authority in Mexico itself, one Nuno de Guzman who in defiance of Cortes wished to seek the northern riches for himself. Far from being able to crush Guzman, Cortes could not even establish a firm order of command between his two ships. The captain of *San Lazaru* was to take his orders from the captain of *La Conception*—or so Cortes ordered.

However, the two ships had scarcely left harbor when the captain of the *San Lazaru* slipped away from his commander to try his own luck. *San Lazaru* did find a new island, but this was inhabited by no more fabulous beings than eagles. There was neither gold nor pearls—nor women. Yet *San Lazaru* was lucky compared to *La Conception*.

The captain of *La Conception*, having first lost half of his command, then lost everything. He was murdered in his sleep by mutineers who had no wish to share their prospective riches with him, Cortes, or the Crown. They then seized control of the ship in a bloody fight. The survivors of the losing side were placed ashore. And *La Conception* headed northwest, away from European authorities, and into the uncharted waters where lay an isle of women and gold.

The mutineers did find a likely looking bay on what could have been (but was not) an island. They found evidence of pearls. But the inhabitants were not black Amazons riding fabulous beasts decked in gold. They were only a people very primitive and very hostile. The landing party was massacred to a man. The skeleton crew that remained on board ship was desperate enough to attempt to sail back to Spanish Mexico.

Here the mutineers finally had a piece of good luck. As chance would have it, they and their ship fell into the hands of Cortes' rival, Guzman; so they were spared. The story of their escapade grew in stature as it traveled in time back to Cortes. What Cortes heard was of disloyal followers, Guzman, and an island of pearls.

Now Cortes could act decisively. There were risks. But Cortes trusted his star, and risks were only mundane things. He would lead the new expedition himself. He would even make provisions for a settlement, after his new conquest.

So Cortes came and saw, but he found nothing worth conquering. He pushed north, and did not find Guzman. He only found what was left of *La Conception* after Guzman had stripped it of everything of worth. He pushed to the northwest, and found the bay where most of the mutineers had been killed. There were indeed pearls, but they were little compensation for the land, a land so dry the natives washed themselves in their urine, so barren they hunted their own feces for edible seeds. Such a people had nothing worth stealing.

And soon the epic theft of plunder was far from even the dreams of Cortes and his men. Soon Cortes and his men were mundanely starving. Even a loyal follower could find nothing enobling about this time. "Of the soldiers that were with Cortes, twenty-three died from hunger and illness; and many others were ill, and they cursed Cortes, his island, his bay, and his discovery."

Even their good luck was bad. When Cortes finally managed to find some food, it resulted in catastrophe. His starved men, despite his warnings, gorged their weakened stomachs. And so fully half of those who had survived the famine died from the feast.

Finally a relief ship arrived from Mexico, to tell Cortes of plots against him there. And so he returned to Mexico. Cortes would find no new lands to plunder to the northwest or anywhere else. His career was now in irretrievable ebb. One of his followers put it well; he said that after the Aztecs "Cortes did not have fortune in anything." Five more years and Cortes would return to Spain to finish his life, dying embittered in the shadows.

One of his lieutenants had wished to call the new land of failure Cortes had discovered, the land where so many of his men died ignominiously, by a simple name: The Cape of Disappointment. But such simplicity was too mild for the curses the soldiers had placed upon it. The name had to be one of contempt, biting contempt for an epic hope misspent. "California," the new land was named, to remind of that fabled isle, that impregnable isle where, amidst abundant women and gold, griffins gorged on hapless men.

California was born in reality as a failure of imagination, a cape of disappointment. Yet that did not deter Spaniards from returning with renewed hope to continue northern exploration in the search for fabled things. No longer did they search for an Amazon isle. Now they looked by land for the seven cities of Cibola, the seven cities of gold: a Spanish friar swore he had seen at least one of them. And they sought by sea the Strait of Anian which Providence had included in creation to ease commerce between the two great oceans of the world: a Greek pilot had sailed its whole length.

Thus it was that more than thirty years before Francis Drake sought haven near the westernmost promontory of the Marin Peninsula, this same promontory had been sighted, and named, by a Spanish expedition. The expedition which Juan Rodriguez Cabrillo led out of New Spain in June, 1542, would be the most extensive European exploration of the California coast in the sixteenth century. This expedition was expected to do more than search for the fabled strait and more than chart the unknown. On such expeditions servants of the Spanish emperor were expected to make periodic landings to take ritual possession of new land on his behalf.

Francisco Ulloa, for instance, the Cortes lieutenant who had suggested the name Cape of Disappointment, had himself been sent on an early reconnaissance of the California coast which prepared for Cabrillo's. When Ulloa would land on a previously unknown portion of the coast, his notary public (brought along for just such occasions) would officially record the following formalities:

"I, Pedro de Palencia, notary public of the fleet, bear witness to all to whose eyes these presents shall come... the very magnificent Senor Francisco de Ulloa... took possession in the name of the Emperor, our master, King of Castille, actually and in reality; placing his hand upon his sword, saying that if any person disputed it he was ready to defend it, cutting trees with his sword, pulling up grass, moving stones from one place to another and from there to another, taking water from the sea and throwing it upon the land, all in token of said possession."

These were the traditional tokens of possession actually and in reality: a threatening touch to the sword hilt, the maiming of a few plants, rocks capriciously moved once and then again, and finally the willful scattering of the sea onto the land. Juan Rodriguez Cabrillo was also expected to follow such formalities periodically. And this

Cabrillo did. Moreover, he seems to have performed this task, like most others assigned to him, with the vehemence to be expected of one who had commanded a company for Cortes in his conquest of the Aztecs. In fact, he named two of the places where he landed "La Posesion," as if to emphasize the effectiveness of his ritualized claim.

The first of these was Puerto de la Posesion, a port discovered in August, 1542, shortly after the expedition had left waters that had been charted by Ulloa. The second was Isla de la Posesion, one of what are now called the Santa Barbara Islands. This was discovered that October, by which time the expedition had made impressive progress, although the Strait of Anian was as yet nowhere to be seen.

Isla de la Posesion marked a change in the expedition; after it there were no more landings because of forbidding coastline and high seas (which were getting progressively worse). On November 14, 1542, the cliffs of Nova Albion were sighted; Cabrillo named the point Cabo de Pinos, after the pines farther back on the ridge. This name did not hold, nor did Drake's Nova Albion. Early in the seventeenth century another explorer in the service of Spain, Sebastian Vizcaino, retraced Cabrillo's path to the Cape of Pines. He, like any explorer, wished to leave his own mark. Whenever he could, he would change Cabrillo's names to ones of his own choosing. When he arrived at the Cape of Pines, the day was the feast of the Epiphany. He renamed the cape after those three kings who in the light of an extraordinary star had given homage to an apparently helpless infant: Punta de Tres Reyes, a name which endured as simply Point Reyes.

The Cabrillo expedition had its own epiphany at Point Reyes, an epiphany as to who finally ruled, not that there was ever any doubt. Within a day after sighting Point Reyes, the Cabrillo expedition was retreating before what one of the crew simply called "frightful seas." The ships retreated further and further south, until finally they sought winter haven in the Santa Barbara Islands. But as they were making their way ashore Cabrillo fell heavily in the surf, shattering a limb which soon became mortally gangrenous. His men buried him on Isla de la Posesion, which they renamed Isla de Juan Rodriguez, another name which did not hold.

In the early twentieth century, there was discovered on one of the Santa Barbara Islands a small flat rock which had some rough carving on it. There is a stick figure of what could be a man; and under it unmistakedly are the letters JR. The carving is conjectured to be a token left by the Spanish crew on that spot of land which took permanent possession of their Juan Rodriguez.

Much of the difficulty of an expedition like Cabrillo's derived from the fact that in going north up the California coast it had to fight prevailing winds and currents. However, in 1564, the very year after Cabrillo's death, the Spaniards found a way to turn this caprice of nature to their advantage.

Since the time of Cortes, the Spaniards had been endeavoring to establish a base in the Orient. The ships Charles V had taken from Cortes for this end had reached the East Indies, but had been lost there. Finally, in 1564, the fifth Spanish expedition to the Orient did succeed in establishing a base on a group of islands which were named after the successor of Charles, Philip II: the Philippines.

By this time the Spanish captains knew that the prevailing easterly winds of the tropics made the voyage from New Spain to the Orient relatively easy. With a base established on the Philippines, what was needed was a route back to the New World; then lucrative trade of the luxuries of the East for the gold and silver of the New World could begin.

The captain who had established a Spanish presence in the Philippines sent his pilot to search for the new route. The pilot sailed his ship north all the way to Japan; there he found prevailing winds which carried his ship back to the New World. More precisely, they carried him to the California coast just to the north of Point Reyes; the currents and winds then carried him southward to Mexico and glory.

Thus began the fabled route of the Manila galleons. The second trip was made in 1566, the third in 1567, the fourth and fifth in 1568. Henceforth every year one, two, as many as three galleons would sail from Manila intending to reach the California coast near Marin, and then follow it to Mexico.

Over the years the range of cargo expanded, but always spices, fabrics, and the exquisite oriental porcelain were staples. The two galleons which arrived in 1573 deposited in "fine gilt china and other porcelain" alone more than 22,000 pieces.

The wealth of this trade was such that it tested even the epic imaginations of the Spanish themselves. The luxury of New Spain

began to startle visitors from the mother country. Manila itself
became an opulent commercial city, the whole economy of
which virtually depended upon the success of the annual galleons.
The profits from having captained a single successful galleon crossing were sufficient to make a man comfortable for life.

The sailings of the galleons were things out of which romances
are written: from the city of Manila—now a city forbidden to all
Europeans not Spanish—from this forbidden oriental city to Mexico,
the land of the Aztecs and Conquistadors. Or rather, the departures
and arrivals were the things out of which romances are written. The
writer of a romance would have to fabricate the voyage itself, for
the actual voyage had little romance in it. Nature had intruded
between the epic departures and arrivals a grisly passage.

It was not so much the navigation up to Japan, although this
could be treacherous. (One pilot grounded his galleon less than a
hundred miles from Manila, and for this mistake was summarily
hung by his crew.) Rather, it was the expanse that opened out before
the galleon when it turned from Japan to the east. That immense
body of water now called the Pacific, these Spaniards, who knew it
more intimately, called simply the Gulf. Galleons entered the gaping
expanse of the Gulf never to be seen again.

The Gulf could be violent. The most opportune season to cross
it also happened to be the time of storms. A galleon as it crossed
the Gulf would be battered by a series of storms, if unlucky by as
many as a dozen. Loss of crew to waves was commonplace; and one
galleon lost six men to lightning alone. But the Gulf did not need to
be violent in order to gorge itself on men. Its very size ordinarily
sufficed; the slow decay of time produced its own cadavers.

Once in the Gulf a galleon's food and water supply soon dete-
riorated. It would not take long for the men to be displaced as the
dominant life forms on their wooden island. The vermin which lived
off them and their stores multiplied, and soon had the run of the ship.

"The Ship swarms with little vermin, the Spaniards call
'Gorgojos', bred in the biscuit; so swift that they in a short time not
only run over the cabins, beds, and the very dishes the men eat on,
but insensibly fasten upon the body. There are several others sorts of
vermin of sundry colors that suck blood. An abundance of flies fall
into the dishes of broth in which there also swim worms of several
sorts."

In such an environment the men, who are daily trying to preserve their ship from the sea, do not remain healthy long. When everyone is ill, only commonly mortal illnesses are worth mentioning. "There are two dangerous diseases in this voyage. Berben swells the body and makes the patient die talking. The other is called the Dutch disease, which makes all the mouth sore, putrefies the gums, and makes the teeth drop out." These quotations are not taken from an early account of a galleon crossing, but from one written after the route had been used for almost a century. Even then, the voyage remained "the longest and most dreadful of any in the world."

Needless to say, few galleons reached New Spain without significant loss of life. Sometimes more than half the crew would perish from disease alone. One ship, the *San Jose*, was sighted off Acapulco over a year after it had left Manila. Yet it did not turn into the harbor. A boat sent from shore to inquire discovered the reason. The *San Jose* was a ghost ship, its opulent cargo intact, its crew putrefying corpses.

These Manila galleons were the first European vessels regularly to sight the Marin Peninsula. They were large ships, some more than a thousand tons. What could the natives have made of these hulks appearing off their coast in an apparent annual migration like the grey whales, yet much rarer than the whales, and dwarfing even them in size? They might have feared them as they feared the grizzly bears and the redwood forests. More likely, they anticipated, as they did with the whales, the rich feast they would have when one finally washed up on their shore.

Of course, first they got not a galleon but Francis Drake and his jackals who had been hunting such slower moving prey. Then there were many speeches, some gifts; but after the initial curiosity had spent itself, the maiden "nochato mu" might well not have been the only person disappointed. After decades of waiting for them to arrive, the visitors had left hardly anything.

Nonetheless, in 1595 one of the great wooden whales finally was beached on the Marin Peninsula. By that time Drake's incursion into Spanish shipping lanes in the Pacific was no longer unprecedented. Thomas Cavendish had taken a Manila galleon off Baja California.

In 1595 Spanish authorities decided to seek a harbor in California where the galleons could replenish their stores and perhaps even pick up an escort for the last leg of the voyage. Chosen to captain the 1595 galleon that left Manila was Sebastian Cermenho, who had been pilot on the vessel that was taken by Cavendish. He was instructed to explore the California coast for a possible site for a Spanish base.

Cermenho's first anchorage after having crossed the gaping Gulf of the Pacific was in fact the bay under Point Reyes, the bay now called Drake's Bay. It was a prudent choice not less for Cermenho than for Drake. Point Reyes protected its bay from the common storms coming out of the northwest.

Cermenho, however, lacked Drake's luck. Soon after he had begun exploring the region in the ship's longboat, a storm blew up from the least likely direction, the southeast. His ship was at the mercy of the elements. With its own sense of humor, the sea, having allowed the ship to cross its gulf with little damage, now destroyed it on the very shores that were supposed to be a haven. Cermenho and his men faced the voyage to Mexico in a longboat, a voyage which must have made even the Gulf crossing seem a pleasure cruise.

The natives of Point Reyes, for their part, seem to have been grateful for their unprecedented gift from the sea. (They had no way of knowing that the price of it would be paid by a city thousands of leaques away.) In the shell mounds of Point Reyes can still be found many shards of the exquisite sixteenth century porcelain the galleon was carrying. And the Point Reyes natives apparently kept these wondrous things for themselves; no sign of such porcelain has yet been found in the shell mounds only a few miles away.

It is likely they did not understand the use for which the delicate teacups and plates were intended. And even if they had been made to understand—perhaps by a Spaniard who in misfortune had retained his sense of humor—they would have found these fragile things unsuited for their life.

They could see that these things, like the beings that brought them, came from a different place, and not just because the things shattered when made to bear the weight of their needs. There were also pictures on the porcelain. Some of the pictures were of things the natives knew, of trees, of deer, of cranes hunting frogs, of spiders hunting flies. But others were of things not of their world, of beings not even to be found in their myths. There were golden fish, birds with dazzling tails longer than themselves, long-headed deer that had wings. There were no evil grizzlies or shrewd coyotes in this land beyond; if there were, surely they would have been pictured, just as they were in the natives' own myths. But there was what seemed

to be a huge lizard with a horrible face not unlike the grizzly—
and this grizzly seemed to hiss fire. Was this the bear of that world,
or the coyote, or the marriage of both?

The answer to such a question could not be divined from the
porcelain itself. Yet these natives had been touched once, and now
again, by that world beyond their own. The porcelain was a token of
that world. And the natives apparently had reverance for that world
and the token which represented it.

Much of the porcelain that survives had been carefully sheared
into smaller pieces. (Of the whole cargo only a single tea cup has
been found intact.) They had been sheared into smaller pieces and
then worked into beads and pendants. The Point Reyes natives
would not trade their gift from the sea. They would rather work
it into shapes they could keep on their persons.

But how did the natives interpret these encounters? Of all their
myths there is but one perhaps related to these initial European
intrusions. This myth tells how, on rare occasions, the spirits of
the dead return to earth, visible. They rise out of the sea of death, and
walk on Point Reyes.

This myth, if it is of that time, contains within it, like most
myths, a deeper truth than its shapers knew. It *was* dead generations
the natives saw wade onto Point Reyes, dead generations of their
people. But it was future death, not past. They were seeing face to
face the extinction of their people. The mournful wailing of the
women, like the myth, held a deeper truth than anyone at that
time knew.

The initial European contacts with the Marin Peninsula, both
sightings and landings, do not constitute a history—or, at best, they
are a fragmented, ironic, ill-shaped history. The English never did
return to occupy, although they impudently persisted in placing
the name Nova Albion on their maps for centuries. (Drake would
have nodded his assent.) The Spanish lost interest in the planned
California galleon base; among other things, they were distracted
by reports of two islands—one rich with gold, the other with silver—
ideally placed somewhere in the midst of the Gulf. (Cortes—the
older Cortes—would only have shaken his head.) The initial European contacts with the Marin Peninsula were isolated incidents
with little significance for the broader course of history, and with no

lasting impact upon the peninsula itself, apart from a few porcelain shards and perhaps a single myth.

So it is that the sixteenth century did not mark the beginning of the recorded history on the Marin Peninsula, but was only a preface to that history, a preface separated from the main text by almost two full centuries. Yet when the Europeans landed once again on the peninsula, those two centuries later, their landing would be no isolated incident. Within another hundred and fifty years, most of the indigenous life of the peninsula, including the native human life, would be displaced, surviving as best it could, if at all, on the unwanted fringes of a European environment. By then the peninsula had been mapped, planted, lumbered, ranched, fenced, roaded, tunneled—in a word, civilized. All this in less than two centuries. And then, at last, it would be decided that Marin should cease to exist as a peninsula at all.

The First Inhabitants
Courtesy of the Bancroft Library

Drake's Bay
Courtesy of the Bancroft Library

II
The Island of the Angels

Europeans finally returned to the Marin Peninsula in August, 1775. The Spanish ship, *San Carlos*, from Mexico entered San Francisco Bay and found safe anchorage off the Marin island now called Angel Island.

The *San Carlos* was also known as *The Golden Fleece*—and this pagan name was, in a way, more appropriate, for the vessel was a Medea with a history of destroying her own children. At the beginning of his journal (the chief surviving account of the voyage), the chaplain, Father Vincente Santa Maria, wrote simply, "She was never to be counted on." Her bad reputation seemed well justified by what the chaplain called merely an "omen of bad luck" at the very beginning of the voyage. "Just as she was getting to open water she ran aground, and as she kept pounding on the sand she was in danger of breaking up. Even the least fainthearted were terror-struck, so many and so great were the alarms that popular rumor scattered about."

The ship was eventually freed, but the incident apparently left the captain the most terror-struck of all. He decided that the sea and his ship were not the only ones conspiring against his leadership. He began to have about his person as many as six loaded pistols, a habit which further disconcerted the already skittish crew. Finally the captain had to be removed from command as "not in his right mind." His position was assumed by his lieutenant, Juan de Ayala. But Ayala himself had to command from bed, for he had accidentally discharged one of the captain's pistols and was seriously wounded in the foot.

The subsequent voyage to San Francisco Bay lacked any comparable incidents, but that did not mean the ship performed well.

25

As Santa Maria put it, "The best that would happen was in one place to escape being wrecked or in another to have a few days relief from danger." But the chaplain was a man of faith, and as the ship approached the Bay of Saint Francis he saw a hand other than Ayala's guiding it.

As the ship approached the entrance of San Francisco Bay, Ayala sent a longboat ahead to find a safe passage for the ship. But the entry into the bay was not to be routine, for at sunset they lost sight of the longboat. Nonetheless, a crescent moon seemed to show the *San Carlos* the way into San Francisco Bay. But as soon as she entered into the bay, winds and strong currents took her to the side of an island, where she suddenly stopped and then began to drift backward. This left Ayala no choice but to cast anchor. Only the next morning did they realize that the change in currents had saved them from shoals which could not be seen in the half-illumined night. Moreover, according to Santa Maria the pilot Ayala sent to find a better anchorage returned to confess he could not. The best place was, in Santa Maria's phrase, "where Providence had placed us."

And not just in the anchorage did Santa Maria find the hand of providence, but also in the people to whom the currents had brought them. These were a handsome people, their leaders friendly to the Spanish, their men protective of their families, their young respectful of their elders. One man gave Santa Maria a string of shells which resembled a rosary; another had painted on his body "a perfect cross." When Santa Maria delivered a short sermon to them ("I knew they could not understand me unless God worked a miracle"), their faces showed "much satisfaction and joy." The natives who were coaxed to board the Spanish vessel were taught to cross themselves and to recite the Pater Noster and the Ave Maria. Once when the chaplain was privately praying, a chief kneeled down beside him and "began to imitate me in my manner of praying so that I could not keep from laughing."

Ayala's own account of the exploration of San Francisco Bay, although brief, presents a more secular version of the same events. "This is certainly a fine harbour: it presents on sight a beautiful fortress, and it has no lack of good drinking water and plenty of firewood and ballast. Its climate, though cold, is altogether beautiful and it is free from such troublesome daily fogs as there are in Monterey, since these scarcely come to its mouth and inside there are very clear days. To these many good things is added the best of all:

the heathen all around this harbour are always so friendly and so docile that I had Indians aboard several times with great pleasure, and the crew as often visited them on land."

The most important record for Ayala was not his or Santa Maria's report but the map of the bay which had been produced. Even here there were differences between Ayala and Santa Maria. Ayala called the island which had given them safety simply The Island of the Angels. Not only had it been a guardian of the ship; but for centuries it had also guarded the bay, for it is this island behind the entrance to the bay that gives the coastline the appearance of being continuous. Father Santa Maria, however, preferred a theologically richer name. Angels, after all, could be good or evil; and even those which were good could be terrible to the sight of men. (Cherubim, for instance, were commonly represented as griffins.) What the chaplain wished to evoke with the name of this island was the assurance that after the Incarnation even the super-human angels submitted to the human. So he evoked the last mystery of the rosary, Mary's coronation as queen of heaven, with his name for the island, Saint Mary of the Angels.

Despite this difference, and despite the fact that Ayala had recorded the date of departure from the new harbor as September 18 and not on the feast of the stigmata of Saint Francis, September 17 (as Santa Maria had), there was one name given by Ayala with which the chaplain must have enthusiastically agreed. The bay to the north of their anchorage Ayala called "Bahia de Nuestra Senora del Rosario, la Marinera," Our Lady of the Rosary, the Mariner—Mary through her rosary commanding not just the angels, but the impersonal sea itself.

Juan de Ayala's landing was not an isolated incident as earlier landings on the Marin Peninsula had been. This expedition was but a part of a larger Spanish expansion into California which had begun six years before. This expansion itself was primarily based upon the plans and aspirations of one man, Jose de Galvez, Inspector General to New Spain.

Jose de Galvez was no swashbuckling Don Quixote, but rather a man of reason and order, a man of the law. His whole career showed that. Indeed, his career was but a part of a broad movement within Spanish government in the eighteenth century, one that attempted to make Spanish government more rational, more uniform, and less dependent upon the vagaries of past history. In Spain itself this meant, among other things, new administrative districts which did not respect the territorial boundaries of the old principalities. No longer could the governor of a province—the intendant, as he was now to be called—perceive himself to be in a direct line to rulers who once had been independent of the crown. His office, his title, his territory were creations of the central government.

When Charles III decided to send an Inspector General to Mexico, central to the mission was the development of a similar reorganization of the Mexican government. No longer would the governor of a province in New Spain be able to envision himself as a latter-day conquistador. He would be clearly just an officer of the crown, a bureaucrat even.

Jose de Galvez was chosen for the office only after one proposed Inspector General declined the offer and another (having been forced to accept) died on the sea voyage. Jose de Galvez, in contrast, flourished in his new office. He hit Mexico like a European storm which had only gained strength as it crossed the Atlantic. Within two years he had devised a complete plan for administrative reorganization. And this was not the only achievement of Galvez. He had also reformed the fiscal affairs. He had established a royal monopoly on tobacco, and tightened measures against smuggling. Galvez exposed and had replaced the Viceroy, who was already suspected in Spain of being both incompetent and dishonest (the Viceroy being one of those who "so admire what is ancient that utter ruin impends").

This was Galvez, the virtuoso administrator. And yet during his Inspectorship a new side to Galvez began to be revealed. The first sign of it came during the expulsion of the Society of Jesus in 1767. The King of Spain had decided that the Jesuit hierarchy of command was a rival to his own. How could the nation and empire be unified if there was an autonomous moral kingdom within its midst? The Jesuits, he ordered, were to be expelled from all Spanish possessions.

In Mexico they were not removed without some trouble. In certain areas close to the capital itself, the native population became rebellious. The Viceroy chose Galvez to lead the troops that were to crush the resistance. Galvez responded with characteristic energy in what appears to have been his first experience with the physical imposition of order. In area after area he rounded-up those suspected of having "hearts full of malice and a desire to do the Spaniards mischief." They were then tried, with himself presiding as judge. Regarding his performance at these trials, Galvez later wrote, "I assure you before God, and with all sincerity, that I have not upon my conscience the slightest scruple of having exceeded the limits of justice, for I mitigated my sentences always with clemency and mercy."

Yet the facts of his judgments do speak for themselves. The people in these areas had caused trouble for the Spanish; there had been some violence, but not a single death was the responsibility of those tried. Nonetheless, in a series of trials, Galvez sentenced six hundred and seventy-four to prison (many for life), banished for life one hundred and seventeen, had seventy-three scourged, and condemned eighty-five to death.

Nonetheless, for once Galvez seems to have been unable to satisfy himself with his own logic. Somehow he needed the punishments to be more than just legal, formally correct; he needed them to be merciful. This need was felt not only in retrospect, but also during the expedition itself. For instance, the following is a report critical of his behavior after passing death sentences at San Luis Potosi.

"As an offset to his violent procedure Galvez assumed a feigned piety, arranging a great funeral pyre, a funeral oration, and all the ceremony with which the greatest heroes might be honored. He added a feature of which it is doubtful if there are many examples; this was to ascend the scaffold himself and harangue the populace, to the accompaniment of tears, a white handkerchief, and exquisite expressions. He then retired to his house to arrange splendid banquets and balls for the following scene, to which he invited all the principal persons of both sexes, and all the officials. With these deeds he was tranquilized, and ready to set out for Guanajuato."

The most penetrating observation of this report is not the charge of hypocrisy, that Galvez was feigning piety, and that his concern was all an act. Rather it is the other, inconsistent observation that Galvez had done all this to tranquilize himself for what still remained to be done. At Guanajuato, for instance, Galvez interviewed six hundred persons in three weeks; he then sentenced one hundred sixty-four to prison (thirty for life), banished eleven, commanded five scourged (two hundred stripes each), sent nine to their death, and personally admonished the more than four hundred others

before freeing them. Galvez must have thought that the variety of
his sentences evidenced his justice and mercy. He made a distinction
even among those condemned. One of the nine would not have his
head stuck on a pike and exposed on a hill overlooking the city.
He at least could go to his death consoled that his loved ones would
not suffer that grisly token of their loss.

Now that Galvez had effected the replacement of the Viceroy,
reformed the fiscal affairs of New Spain, formulated the correct plan
for its new centralized administration, and supervised both the
expulsion of the Jesuits and the eradication of other disorderly elements, there remained for him just one major task.

In his administrative reorganization Galvez had recognized the
peculiar problems presented by the northern frontier provinces.
The north presented no neat boundaries; it was a gaping, open space,
sparsely settled, and at a great distance from the capital. Thus, in
his plan Galvez allowed more autonomy to that local governor.
Always sensitive to formalities, Galvez recommended that he be
called a Commandant rather than an Intendant. The position would
be a difficult one. The Commandant would have to bring order
where little or none had existed before. His function would be more
like that of Galvez than of the new Viceroy. In fact, in order to
prepare the ground for the new Commandant, Jose de Galvez would
personally go to the north.

This decision was justified to the king on strategic grounds.
The one potential weakness in the Spanish American Empire—
indeed, of the Spanish dominance of the Pacific—was its northern
Mexican frontier, particularly the California coast. If a Nova Albion,
or some such colony, was effectively established in the north by
Britain, or Russia, or perhaps France, it would constitute a continuing threat to Spanish security, a threat that would dwarf the
harrassment that Spanish shipping suffered from the occasional
foreign pirate.

So the decision for a northern expedition was a rational one.
And the decision that Galvez, despite his general lack of military
experience, should command it was also reasonable. He was, after
all, the highest-ranking official behind the viceroy; and he, unlike the
viceroy, could be spared from the day-to-day administrative affairs.

And yet Galvez seemed to take more than his usual pleasure
in the assignment. As he traveled north, he seemed in fact almost
euphoric. Ordinarily he could find some fault with any administra-

tion; his genius was to find fault, and then to find ways—the correct ways—to remedy the fault. Nonetheless, at Guadalajara, on May 2, 1768, the feared Galvez pronounced the local administration all but perfect, and recommended generous raises for a number of officials. Who was he to nitpick with the great work before him?

This work was in a way the culmination of his career. He had begun in Spain as a lawyer who worked effectively within a system both he and his opponents, both his superiors and his clients, all had to accept as given. As such he gained the attention of the crown by brilliantly winning a case against it on behalf of foreign interests. When the king, always sensitive to matters of national loyalty, questioned his judgment for even taking such a case, Galvez is supposed to have replied, "My Lord, the law is greater even than the King." His Lord subsequently appointed Galvez to the important assignment as his unyielding Inspector General. As such Galvez was no longer just an instrument of a pre-existing order, but rather he was also an instrument of its reform; in New Spain Jose de Galvez was to make that order more rational. Then came the rebellion of 1767, and Galvez found himself capable of physically imposing his order on those who challenged it. Now in 1768 Jose de Galvez was bringing human order where none had existed before; he had the opportunity to be virtually the creator of this order, *ex nihilo.*

Galvez's plan for the Sacred Expedition, as the Spanish thrust into California was called, had a rational simplicity typical of him. There would be four major contingents, two by land, two by sea. They would make their individual ways to San Diego harbor. The prominent members of the expedition would be rationally distributed. The doctor of the expedition, the noted Pedro Prat, would be assigned to the first sea contingent, to see to any cases of scurvy that might develop on board, and also to be at San Diego to offer his assistance if needed when the other contingents arrived. Gaspar de Portola and Junipero Serra, the respective military and spiritual leaders of the expedition, would be in the second land contingent, and hence would be able to follow the trail blazing of the first and would arrive in San Diego after the port had been secured.

After a mission and fort had been established in San Diego, one land contingent and at least one sea contingent would continue north and establish a fort and mission at the harbor of Monterey. Then some of the Monterey group would return south and choose a site for a third mission half way between the other two. Upper

California would then be Spain's. The expedition, moreover, would not have to worry about supplies, for after the last land contingent had left Baja California, Galvez would send a supply ship to the outposts, just to be safe.

To make preparations for the expedition to upper California, Jose de Galvez crossed by ship from Mexico to the peninsula of Baja California, the very peninsula where centuries earlier Cortes had come to grief. When Galvez saw the arid waste of the peninsula, he grieved also.

The missions here were supposed to provide the base for northward expansion. Yet for all the money, men, and directives Spain had sent here, he found no semblance of civilized order. The missions were "mere farms," the natives simply "vagrants searching for roots, seeds, fruits, and animals." This, after those in charge had had enough time, enough money, and the right rules for making civilized and happy the natives entrusted to their care.

Having found no order, Galvez set about to impose it. The military had clearly mismanaged the material affairs of the mission colonies; the mission administration was to be centralized in the hands of the missionaries. (The soldiers who had been notably incompetent or dishonest were to be given a chance to make amends; they would be selected for the expedition that would be going to upper California.) The population of the natives was irrationally distributed on the peninsula, the greatest concentrations being precisely in the places least suitable for agriculture; the missionaries in those places were to round up a suitable proportion of their charges to send them, under guard if necessary, to where they would want to go if they were rational.

Galvez did not have his way with this recommendation, nor with some of the many others he proposed to the missionaries which they believed would only scare away prospective converts. There was, however, one policy about which he was adamant: the natives must be *clothed*. In his dispatches he returns again and again to the same theme. "The total nakedness in which the men and women have lived did not, either in the former or the latter, permit the modesty to arise which is the first motor of all the actions and virtues in rational beings who know it and have it." A precondition for all the other improvements which Galvez envisaged was that the native be taught to "clothe himself like a rational being."

There was an irony to Jose de Galvez's insistence on clothing. Galvez was making his demands to the missionaries, and these missionaries were followers of Francis of Assisi. The juxtaposition itself was striking: Jose de Galvez and Francesco d'Assisi, the man of reason and the man of faith, the administrator and the saint. And this was no ordinary saint, but a saint of nakedness. He had once preached naked as a penitent. When he was dying, he had himself stretched on the bare ground naked, so that he might leave the world as humbly as he had entered it. This was the saint whose followers were supposed to help Galvez clothe the natives so that they might be rational.

Rationalism Francis never preached. His kingdom of God, unlike Galvez's empire of Spain, was a place of inspired madness. Why else would Francis kiss lepers? When Francis called one of his earliest disciples, Brother Juniper, "God's fool," he was giving the highest praise. "Would I had a forest of such junipers." And Francis, from his own time down to the eighteenth century, did in fact have such a forest of Franciscans. The Friars Minor, in particular, were to be a forest of men whose view of the world had been nurtured by stories of the life of Francis, such as the collection called *The Little Flowers.*

Typical of these stories is the one in which Francis taught Brother Leo where perfect joy was. One winter day, according to the story, Francis and Leo were walking to Saint Mary of the Angels, the church most cherished by Francis and his friars; his first divine call had been to repair this church. As they walked, Francis began to proclaim where perfect joy was not. It was not to be found in being an exemplar of "holiness, integrity, and good edification." It was not to be found in miraculous cures for suffering. It was not to be found in knowledge, either knowledge of "the future or of the secrets of the consciences and minds of others." Nor was it to be found in the knowledge of "the courses of the stars, the powers of herbs and . . . the qualities of birds and fishes, animals, humans, roots, trees, rocks, and waters."[1]

Francis had, according to the story, been continuing in this vein for more than two bitterly cold miles. Brother Leo had remained entirely silent; presumably he was content with knowing where imperfect joy could be found, within the shelter and warmth of Saint

Mary of the Angels. Then, finally, Francis managed to exasperate even the freezing Leo.

"Brother Leo, even if a Friar Minor could preach so well that he should convert all the infidels to the faith of Christ, write that perfect joy is not there."

"Father I beg you in God's name to tell me where perfect joy is."

"When we come to Saint Mary of the Angels, soaked by the rain and frozen by the cold, all soiled with mud and suffering from hunger"—Brother Leo must have been a bit disappointed; he had known all along—"and we ring at the gate of the place and the brother porter comes and says angrily: 'Who are you?' And we say 'We are two of your brothers.' And he contradicts us, saying: 'You are not telling the truth. Rather you are two rascals who go around deceiving people and stealing what they give to the poor. Go away!' And he does not open for us, but makes us stand outside in the snow and rain, cold and hungry, until night falls—then if we endure all those insults and cruel rebuffs patiently, without being troubled and without complaining, and if we reflect humbly and charitably that this porter really knows us and that God makes him speak against us, oh, Brother Leo, write that perfect joy is there!"

Perfect joy Francis found in "conquering oneself and willingly enduring sufferings, insults, and humiliations, and hardships for the love of Christ." This perfect joy came only after one relinquishes any claim to superiority over any of God's creatures. Then alone can one selflessly enter into the hymn of praise that all creation sings. Brother Sun sings it, as do Sisters Moon and Stars. Brothers Wind and Air sing, and also Brother Fire, full of power and strength. Sings it too Sister Earth, our mother, and Sister Water as well. All praise the Lord, even "Sister Death from whose embrace no mortal can escape."

Franciscans, men enthused with such divine madness, men who courted Sister Death and Holy Martyrdom, who embraced poverty and kissed disease, who counted a humiliation as an occasion for joy—such men could be of use to a Jose de Galvez, who was nobody's fool. He first used them as docile replacements for the unruly Jesuits in lower California. Attracted by danger and hardship, they would not regard assignment to the expedition to upper California as a punishment. Their presence would even permit Galvez to finance the expedition largely out of the Pious Fund; New Spain would secure its most vulnerable border through charitable contributions.

In all this Galvez had calculated shrewdly. The irrational landscape of California was indeed a promised land for the true Franciscans. This was a vale of tears in which they could find all the penance they could wish. They could be like the cypresses which flourish on the serpentine soil that thwarts other trees.

And Galvez had indeed met in Baja California a true follower of Francis, a juniper that would flourish on the serpentine, Junipero Serra. The first name was no happy coincidence. Serra, baptized Miguel, had selected Junipero as his religious name when he entered the Franciscan order because Brother Juniper had been, in Serra's words, "the greatest exemplar of holy simplicity."

Many of Serra's early years as a Friar Minor showed the difficulty of maintaining this ideal of holy simplicity, even within the Franciscan order. Francis had, for instance, forbidden his brothers to possess books. The Friars Minor were to be, as their name suggested, less than everyone else. Yet how could they be less if they knew more? This was one of the founder's strictures—one of the many—that was overturned during his own lifetime. And in the century after his death in 1226 the Franciscan Order of Friars Minor produced many of the most sophisticated philosophers and theologians of Christendom.

By the eighteenth century the path was well-trod. Brother Junipero soon became Father Junipero, then earned his doctorate in theology, and finally accepted the call to a distinguished professorship of philosophy at one of the great universities of Spain. There was even recorded part of a petty dispute whether the new professor Serra or another should take academic precedence in examinations. The original Brother Juniper would not have understood it, but Inspector General Galvez would not have found it hard.

Nonetheless, the Franciscan spirit was far from dead within Serra. Perhaps it was reawakened by the woman who shouted at him during one of his sermons, "Rant on, rant on, but you will be dead before the end of Lent." Whatever the proximate causes, the next year Junipero Serra and his student Francisco Palou applied to their superiors to be assigned to the foreign missions. So it was that in 1748, at the age of thirty-five, Junipero Serra arrived in New Spain. And he had scarcely been in this new land a month when he received a special grace from God.

Francis of Assisi himself had received his own greatest grace near the end of his life, a grace which as far as is known was given to no human before. At the top of Mount Alverna, during one of his frequent and increasingly severe penitential vigils, Francis witnessed a miracle. A flaming seraph administered to him the Stigmata. Francis had become so Christ-like that he was allowed to live the last days of his life with Christ's own wounds on his body.

Serra's grace was of a humbler kind. He had come to the New World to be a most literal Franciscan, more literal than his Order had been. Francis in the earliest surviving rule for his Order had included the injunction that a friar "must not ride on horseback unless compelled by the manifest necessity or infirmity." This was one of the very first Franciscan injunctions to be compromised. (And the last head of the Franciscan friars who had walked Europe to visit his brothers, John of Parma, was himself imprisoned by his successor as a heretic.) But the first decision Serra made in the New World was to obey it.

When Serra and his fellow missionaries arrived in Mexico, weakened by a difficult three-month voyage, they still faced an arduous journey overland to the Franciscan house in Mexico City. Of the almost two dozen missionaries, only Serra and one other, he perhaps under Serra's influence, insisted upon risking their safety by walking the distance. Serra had come to the New World to abandon himself to Divine Providence. He would start now.

Twice during this arduous trek Serra and his companion were saved from difficulty by what Serra interpreted to be a saintly intercession. Yet neither of these intercessions, extraordinary as they were, was the greatest grace Serra received. Junipero Serra, on this very first walk in the new land that he prayed would provide the site for his martyrdom, received his own stigma. No flaming seraph administered the wound, as had administered the five wounds to Francis on Mount Alverna. Serra, it seems, was simply bitten by a mosquito. He scratched at the bite during his sleep; it festered, and for the rest of his life he suffered from an ulcerous leg, suffered greatly though joyfully.

When Jose de Galvez arrived in Baja California in 1769, he found Junipero Serra the new president of the California missions. By this time Serra had already distinguished himself as a missionary. In Mexico he had converted the Parmes who had resisted Christianity for centuries. He had achieved this conversion less by his learning than by his example. When Serra preached penance to his parishioners, he flagellated himself for their sins until they cried for him to stop. At the head of a procession on Good Friday, Serra carried a cross stronger men could not lift. When, in desperation, the pagans put poison in his sacramental wine to be rid of him, Serra let the poison run its course lest the antidote cause him to vomit.

After his success with the Parmes, Serra was ready for the most rigorous assignment his Order could give him. At first this was to be in Texas. There was an uprising of infidels who—led, it was said, by cannibals—martyred two missionaries, one of whom had traveled to the New World with Serra. Serra was overjoyed to be chosen to follow on the same path, but the military who were to accompany him began to have prudent thoughts. The expedition was postponed, and Serra was assigned to replace the Jesuits in the strategically more important Baja California. If the friar was intent upon shedding his blood, let him do so where both the glory of God *and* the security of the empire would be optimally served.

Serra had chosen himself to be the spiritual leader of the Sacred Expedition. No one else would have chosen him, and not just because he was now almost sixty years of age. All the activity in preparation for the expedition had left Serra's leg in a frightful condition. When Palou saw the leg shortly before Serra left, "I could not keep back my tears." When Serra said farewell "till I see you in Monterey, where I hope that we shall come together again to work in that vineyard of the Lord," all Palou could reply was "Until eternity." And so Father Serra had to lecture his old student for his lack of faith.

The expedition had not progressed very far before Serra was in such agony he could neither stand nor sit—nor even sleep. Gaspar de Portola, the military leader of the expedition, pleaded with him to allow himself to be carried back. Serra was adamant. "Even if I die on the road I will not go back, but you can bury me here and I shall very gladly remain among these pagan people if such be the will of God for me."

Portola was a pragmatist. He knew he could not reason with Serra on the subject; coercing him would be more trouble than it was worth. Therefore, he had to be humored. And so they humored him as they traveled while he grimaced on his stretcher. And they humored him when he asked the muleteer to treat his leg as he would a mule's. And they must have been amazed when the treatment was successful. Serra would not have been amazed, thankful but not amazed. He was a follower of Francis of Assisi. And Francis had a name for his own body. He called it Brother Ass.

At this very time Jose de Galvez was suffering his own trial. During the immediate preparations for the expedition he had at times seemed almost giddy with excitement. When one of the sea contingents of the expedition finally was ready to embark, Galvez first preached to them what he himself called a "homily a la burlesca."

"It will be said that in California there is verified la comedia del Diablo Predicator, and I shall laugh that so they call me, if only we gain the blessed object of our enterprise. . . . But the tongue, in my preachments, only spoke the feelings of my heart, which had gone in the ships, I not being able myself to go with them."

After the expedition had left, Galvez himself had to leave Baja California. A rebellion of natives had begun in northern Mexico. If this area was lost to Spanish control, the whole California advance would be jeopardized. Galvez had made the patron saint of the California expedition San Jose, Saint Joseph, the Holy Patriarch, "my saint." Now it was in his hands; Galvez would face his own trial putting down the unruly natives in Sonora.

He had to put them down, but somehow he could not, no matter how ruthless the methods he employed. He seemed to be failing. Yet he, Jose de Galvez, could not fail; it could not be his fault. If there was a failure, it was not due to him or the order of which he was but an instrument. The spent Galvez began to hear voices, voices sent by God whispering to him which of his subordinates were betraying him—Francis of Assisi, among others, became Galvez's personal informant.

Then at last Galvez began to realize that he was not who people thought he was. He was a king—no, he was San Jose, the Holy Patriarch—no, no, he was God Himself, the Eternal Father. That he might be recognized for who he was, he burned his clothes and appeared before his men to administer the Last Judgment, naked.

His subordinates could keep secret his condition no longer. They wrote to Mexico City. Jose de Galvez had lost "that which in other times had caused wonder in all who consulted him"; he had lost his "beautiful reason." Galvez himself in a moment of lucidity had written on a slip of paper: "Jose de Galvez, insane for the un-happy world, pray God for him that he may be happy in the next."

If the insane Galvez had known what was happening to his elegant plan, this alone might have been enough to drive him over the brink. He already had a glimpse of its fate when word came to him in Sonora that the supply ship, named by Galvez *San Jose,* had after two months at sea limped back into harbor with a broken mast. Galvez ordered it refitted and sent out again. It went back to sea, never to be seen again, neither ship nor crew nor even wreckage.

The fate of the *San Carlos,* now to begin to earn her reputation as a Medea, was little better. When the *San Carlos* finally arrived in San Diego harbor after four gruesome months at sea, almost all on board left alive were desperately ill. The scurvy was so bad it was like a plague. Soon the crew of the second ship, which had reached San Diego before the unseaworthy *San Carlos,* succumbed to the disease as well. While they waited for the land contingents to arrive, Pedro Prat performed heroically in setting up a tent hospital and ministering to the sick, as the entry in the diary of one crewman makes clear.

"These measures, however, were not sufficient to restore their health; for medicines and fresh food, most of which had been used up during the voyage, were wanting. The surgeon, Don Pedro Prat, supplied this want as far as possible, with some herbs which he sought with much trouble in the fields and whose properties he knew. He himself needed them as much as his patients, for he was all but prostrated by the same disease as they. In the barracks the cold made itself severely felt at night, and the sun by day: extremes which caused the sick to suffer cruelly. Every day, two or three of them died, and the whole expedition, which had been composed of more than ninety men, was reduced to only eight soldiers and as many sailors who were in a condition to assist in guarding the ships, handling the launches, protecting the camp, and waiting upon the sick."

When Portola finally arrived three months later, the ordeal was not over. Although neither of the land parties had suffered significant losses, they had nothing which would relieve the suffering of the seamen. From both crews Portola could piece together but a single skeleton crew which might survive the sea journey back to Baja California for additional supplies and reinforcements. Prat would have to do the best he could until the *San Jose* arrived. Portola would spare only Serra and another friar and half a dozen able-bodied soldiers for a guard.

Portola had vowed in Baja California that he would fulfill his assigned mission or die in the trying. It was not that Portola cherished martyrdom. He had been military governor of Baja California, and the military administration there had been severely criticized by the powerful Galvez. If Portola failed in upper California too, his future would be worth little.

Portola, whatever the risk, was going to push north to Monterey with the rest of the able-bodied soldiers, and the two remaining friars. When the *San Jose* arrived and had given Prat and the sick what assistance it could, the ship with Serra was to continue to Monterey to give support to Portola as well. By the time Portola returned, San Diego should have received reinforcements from the ship Portola had sent back to Baja.

About six months later, when Portola and his men straggled back into San Diego (reeking of the mule meat which alone had preserved them from starvation on the last stage of the march), Prat and Serra were still waiting for those two ships. For six months Prat had been losing a man a week to scurvy, and Serra himself was now suffering from it.

But Serra had even worse news for Portola. The natives, for the sake of whose souls the Sacred Expedition had been undertaken, had turned hostile. They had attacked, and barely been repulsed. Serra could only thank God for this, and especially for the fact that none of the unbaptized natives themselves had been killed.

Even up to the attack, Serra's missionary efforts had been a failure. He had in fact almost baptized one infant. Yet in the midst of the ceremony the natives suddenly snatched it away from him, and ran away. A few more seconds and it would have been a Christian. The fault was his, Serra's fault. God was punishing him for some sin. And now an immortal soul may have been lost forever because of it.

When Serra told Portola this story of the aborted baptism, he almost certainly wept; years later whenever he retold the story he would weep. As for Portola, he likely waited until later to query his men privately about the attack. How could they repel such a dangerous attack without killing some of the savages? And had they become such bad shots since he left? The response is not hard to imagine.

Well, they had wounded some, whom the good Doctor Prat eventually treated when things quieted down. They had also, if the truth be known, killed a number. The friars had spent the fight praying in their tent. So the friars never really saw what happened. And after it was over the men thought it better to keep this particular piece of news from them, especially from Father Serra.

Some such exchange, out of Serra's hearing, likely took place between Portola and his men after his return. In the official reports of the expedition, the number of native wounded and dead are estimated to be the same. And Junipero Serra went to his grave thanking God that no natives had been killed.

Native dead were the least of Portola's worries in his circumstances. Not only had the supply ships failed to arrive (which alone would make his position at San Diego tenable), Portolo himself had failed to find Monterey Bay. The *San Jose* might well be sitting there still waiting for him. "You have returned from Rome without seeing the Pope," said Serra—which could not have helped.

Portola had in fact found Monterey; he had just failed to see it. Portola lacked imagination, and did not understand it in others. The contrast between his diary and that of the Franciscan who was accompanying him, Friar Crespi, was striking. The Franciscan recorded many marvels: tremblings of the earth, ferocious bears, huge reddish trees, mountains so steep goats could not climb them, a friendly native the soldiers dubbed "El Loco." But the Franciscan was always looking for God's wonders. When Portola looked at a landscape, he was interested only in how long it would take to traverse, and whether or not it would provide water and pasturage. A Pedro Prat might fret himself away over the sick; a Portola only acknowledges their existence when the expedition is delayed to give them the last rites.

When Portola arrived at Monterey Bay, he consulted the description of it he had been given, a description that was almost two centuries old and made by an explorer who was inclined to exaggerate the importance of his own discoveries. That nature might have rearranged the bay, or that the previous explorer might have improved upon what he saw, neither of these possibilities occurred to Portola. His orders explicitly directed him to establish a Spanish presence on Monterey Bay, for which he had an explicit description. This bay did not fit the description. This bay was not Monterey. The expedition must continue north.

Portola realized that they had passed Monterey when from a hill he saw Point Reyes in the distance. Some of his party also thought they saw a ship at anchor under it. It must be the *San Jose* come to give them succor. Portola did not see the ship, but he did see a large inland body of water connected to the ocean. Crespi also saw it and described it as a "very large and fine harbor, such that not only all the navy or our most Catholic majesty but those of all Europe could take shelter in it." Crespi can be forgiven his exaggeration. So too can Portola be forgiven for perceiving one of the great natural harbors of the world as merely an "arm of the sea" which was in his way.

Portola was consoled by the fact that they had obviously passed Monterey, and hence did not have to continue to the north. (The *San Jose*, if it was there, would have to fend for itself.) Portola and his men retraced their steps to Monterey Bay. The bay had not changed in the meantime; neither had the description Portola carried with him. He was at a loss to think where else to look for the perfect harbor of Monterey. He admitted failure and returned to San Diego.

Now he was faced with another decision. How long should he wait for one of the relief ships to arrive? *San Jose* should have been at San Diego long before now. And the crew of the other ship were sickly even before they left; perhaps they had not made it back. (He would later learn that most of this crew had in fact died of scurvy during the voyage, and the ship had been virtually helpless when it arrived; a few more deaths and it would have arrived as a ghost ship, if it arrived at all.)

In making his decision, Portola seems to have tried to strike a balance between any of his men who were for immediately turning back and the friars who were content to be buried there. Portola would wait until March 19, the feast of Saint Joseph, patron saint of the Sacred Expedition. If the Holy Patriarch was not going to save the Sacred Expedition by then, Portola would have to try to salvage what he could of it by himself. Saint Joseph, even the friars should admit, thus far had not been exactly a good provider.

Serra knew well enough what a return might mean. It had been almost two hundred years since the Spanish had been on this coast. It might be another two hundred years before they would try again. That would deprive generations of natives from even the possibility of Christianity. Portola might wish to keep God to a time-table.

Serra would do no such thing. He would stay in San Diego until the end.

Serra was perfectly willing to be martyred. He and another friar would stay, as he put it in his diary, "until the last breath." Conversion in the eighteenth century, no less than in the first, sprang from soils watered by martyrs' blood.

Serra was as simple as a dove, but he also had a little serpentine wisdom. Serra knew how to use his willingness to be martyred as a tool to influence those who did not want to feel even indirectly responsible for his blood. After Serra and the other friar had made their martyrs' decision, he presented it to the captain of the remaining ship. The captain was persuaded to remain in harbor after Portola left with the land party, for a while at least.

Perhaps Serra hoped to use the captain to influence Portola to relent as well. If he did, he misjudged Portola. Portola saw things, as always, plainly. If God or Saint Joseph wished to intervene on behalf of the Sacred Expedition, far be it from Gaspar de Portola not to give them enough time to get around to it. He would even give them an appropriate occasion, the feast of Saint Joseph. As for the friars, he would allow them to use whatever ritualistic means were at their disposal to achieve this intervention. He would allow Serra to give a novena in preparation for the feast. What else could the soldiers do to speed the ship on its way but pray? Nonetheless, if the ship, *any* ship did not come after all that, he was leading his men back. Failure was one thing; suicide another.

So the feast of Saint Joseph arrived, shipless. As its solemnities were being observed, Serra must have been preparing himself to be left behind, recounting to himself his many sins that deserved this abandonment; Portola must have been thinking through the route back, the easy and difficult parts of the terrain, where there was water and pasturage; Prat must have been grieving about how many more he must lose, how little his efforts had come to; and one sea captain might well have been quietly cursing himself for having melted in the face of sanctity.

The feast of Saint Joseph came, and before vespers the relief ship was seen in San Diego harbor. It had not meant to come here. It had tried to make its way to Monterey, but had turned back when it had inexplicably lost an anchor. Portola himself admitted that the Sacred Expedition had been saved by the intervention of Saint Joseph. The natives were not Junipero Serra's only mission.

With the arrival of the relief ship, the Sacred Expedition was saved. Portola now made a new attempt to find Monterey, one contingent by sea, one by land. This time Serra went, and this time Portola recognized Monterey when he saw it. A mission and fort were established in Monterey in June, 1770.

Within five years the decision had been made to occupy the southern peninsula created by that arm of the sea in which all the navies of Europe could be harbored. The Ayala expedition was, as Santa Maria's journal implies, more than just a voyage of exploration. The year before, a land route from Sonora to Upper California had been opened. The Viceroy wished to use it to transport a group of colonists from Mexico to San Francisco which he intended to occupy with both a mission and a fort. So at the same time Ayala's ship was making her way up the California coast, a party of thirty-four families, thirty of them headed by soldiers, was proceeding to California via land. They would not reach Monterey until the next year. Ayala's exploration was in part to prepare for the arrival of these settlers.

Ayala's expedition was sent to reconnoiter the bay, while others were sent to explore by land. The Marin Peninsula was about to become the southernmost portion of the California coast not under direct Spanish control. The island of the angels and the bay of our mariner lady of the rosary would remain for a time just beyond the reach of the Spanish king.

At the time Ayala's ship entered the bay, Junipero Serra was president of the California missions which numbered five and had almost five hundred native converts. He had recently returned from Mexico where he had arranged to have the governor of California removed; the governor had attempted to thwart Serra's efforts to establish more missions. Serra was a saint with whom one did not test strength. The life had been hard; one winter they had survived only on bear meat the soldiers had provided by hunting. But the life was no harder than Serra himself. When he heard that one of his missionaries had been killed by the natives in San Diego, he is supposed to have said: "Thanks be to God; now that the terrain has been watered by blood, the conversion of the San Diego natives will take place." When a native implicated in this murder was dragged from the mission church to be incarcerated, Serra upheld the excommunication of the officer who had ordered it.

Shortly after the founding of Monterey, Serra's Franciscan superior in Mexico had written, "It will be necessary to restrain his ardent zeal to some extent." That zeal would remain ardent to the end of his life. He never had enough missions or missionaries or converts; there was always more to do, and more suffering to endure joyfully for the sake of the doing. Serra would die in 1784. His last recorded words would be, "Now let us go to rest."

Portola, in contrast to Serra, left California as soon as he could, literally by the first ship back to Mexico. Saint Joseph or no, he knew better than to press his luck; let one of his lieutenants take over as military commander of wonderful California. He received a hero's welcome in Mexico City; his career was made. Yet he had no affection for the land which had reluctantly permitted this. He recommended that Spain allow whichever of its enemies that wishes to attempt to settle California; the suffering they will endure will be greater punishment of their ambition than any that could be inflicted by Spanish arms. By 1775 Gaspar de Portola had returned to Spain. Eventually he would take his pension and die in his native land, an old man, comfortable in his place.

As for the good doctor, Pedro Prat, he alone of the three was no longer alive in 1775. He had gone with the sea contingent in the successful expedition to found Monterey in 1770. His worst ordeal, it seemed, was over; but that proved not to be so. The Sacred Expedition had been too much for him. As Serra put it in a letter, "No sooner was the port of Monterey found than the surgeon lost his mind." For a year they confined him in the fort, and prayed for him in the mission. To no avail; he was "completely deranged." He was sent back to Mexico to an asylum where he went to his rest in 1771.

Mission San Rafael Archangel
Courtesy Marin County Historical Society

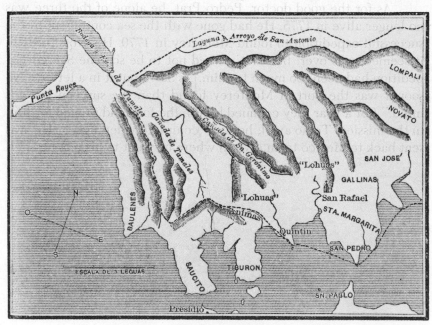

Marin in 1834
Courtesy of the Bancroft Library

III
The Mission of Saint Raphael

The landing on Angel Island in 1775 had represented an end to Marin's almost two century isolation from European contact. Within a year there would be both a mission and a fort on the San Francisco Peninsula. For the natives it must have been an extraordinary time. They were seeing strange things, and they could ponder anew old stories based on older memories, stories of the dead emerging from the sea to walk Point Reyes.

For a time the Indians had only to observe and ponder. When Junipero Serra himself was brought to the tip of the San Francisco Peninsula in 1775, he looked across at Marin and exclaimed: "Thanks be to God! Our Father Saint Francis with the Holy Cross of the mission procession has reached the end of the California continent; for to pass beyond he must embark."

For the twenty-five years after the founding of San Francisco the attention of the Franciscans was fixed on the mission procession as it extended from San Diego to San Francisco. San Francisco remained a northern beachhead. The new northern missions were established to connect San Francisco with Monterey, not to extend further the procession.

Only after 1800 would Spanish exploration parties regularly touch Marin soil. And only after 1800 do Marin names become frequent in the San Francisco baptismal record. Then, on December 13, 1817, the friars finally embarked to pass beyond what Serra had taken to be the California continent. They embarked to extend the mission procession.

The prefect of the missions, Serra's successor, Fra Sarria, was in the party with three other Franciscans; Arbella, the commander of the San Francisco fort, accompanied them, along with a small mili-

tary guard. They sailed across the bay to a good anchorage half-way
up the Marin Peninsula. A mile or two inland from that point, at the
base of a small hill, on the side of a fertile valley, at a place the
natives told them was called Nanagauni, they planted the cross,
symbol of the tree on which Christ died and through which all men
could be redeemed. They planted the cross, and sang *Te Deum*.

> You God we praise.
> You Lord we acclaim.
> You the eternal Father
> All creation worships.

They sang stanza after stanza, as had Serra decades before at Monterey, and before that at San Diego. They sang it, as he did, through
its stanzas of praise to its concluding stanza of petition.

> Come then Lord, and help your people,
> Saved by the sacrifice of your own blood,
> And bring us with your saints
> To glory everlasting.

Serra almost half a century before had petitioned for a procession of missions. And now in 1817 the procession was there; this
mission would be the twenty-first. You God we praise. These missions had had tens of thousands of converts; they had had their
apostles and their martyrs. You God we acclaim. And now here, in
another pagan place another mission would be founded, this one
sanctified by the name San Rafael. You the Eternal Father all creation worships.

But the trip to Nanagauni—soon to be baptized San Rafael—
had been long. It was dusk when they arrived. So they planted the
cross, had vespers, sang a Te Deum, and then they retired. The formal founding of San Rafael would have to wait until the morning's
light, a new day for a new mission.

Although San Rafael was only to be, at least initially, a branch
of San Francisco, Sarria would perform that next morning the full
rite for the founding of an independent mission. Sarria's decision
was undoubtedly based on a number of considerations. Formal ritual
always attracted the natives to a new mission. (And that next day,
after the dedication, there was recorded a number of baptisms.)
The ritual was also a sign of respect for the zeal of Fra Gil, who
would be left behind to man this mission outpost alone; the violence
of the natives of this region was well known, and Gil was clearly
risking a lonely martyrdom. And there was also, if truth be known,

Prefect Sarria's own convenience as a busy administrator; if San Rafael produced not a martyr but a flock, then Sarria, already having performed the ceremony, could make it an independent mission by messenger.

Nonetheless, there was another reason for performing the full rite. None of the Spaniards there, including Sarria himself, had ever seen it performed. The last time it had been performed in California had been more than a decade before. To perform it again would mark a new morning for the California missions. It would be to say that there would be new mornings once again, many new mornings.

The dedication of San Rafael was for the Franciscans there the expression of a hope, the making of a petition. But Sarria's petition, unlike Serra's decades before, would not be granted. It was now eventide in Serra's vineyard, time for vespers and then repose. Come then, Lord, and help your people.

As the boat carrying Sarria and the others first approached its Marin anchorage, it must have passed near, if not through, sea otter herds. The herds were said to be so thick in that portion of the bay, they made it glisten black. Perhaps Sarria, looking at the playful otters, wondered at God's providence which uses all creatures great and small, thinking and unthinking. This might well have occurred to him, for the otter as much as the Franciscan was responsible for the founding of Mission San Rafael. Sarria could not have done it without him.

Sarria's dependence on the otter to found even a small mission might seem strange given the obvious successes of the California mission system since the days of Serra. The missions had become virtually self-sufficient units. The number of neophytes had grown to twenty thousand; harvest of grain had reached one hundred thousand bushels annually; sheep and cattle now numbered in the hundreds of thousands. Sarria seemed to have at his command the material resources of a kingdom.

The coyote and grizzly certainly thought so, and each tried to share in it in its own way. Coyotes were forever lurking about the missions looking for their chance. One visitor to San Francisco in the 1820s was amazed to find the coyote "so daring and dextrous that it had no scruple of entering human habitation in the night, and rarely fails to appropriate whatever happens to suit it." The grizzlies, in contrast, were not creatures of stealth. They simply hunted the livestock, and became such a problem in one northern mission that a grizzly was killed almost every other week. The grizzlies had to learn that the mission lands, despite the easy prey, were really death traps; the coyote did not have to learn such guile, for it had long lived with the grizzly.

The ample food supply of the missions, while attracting varmints and predators to them, also attracted immortal souls. These immortal souls were so immired in their fallen natures that the temporal resources of the mission had to be used, in the phrase of one friar, as "the bait and means for spiritual fishing." Without such inducements the natives "would not obey or love that which is preached to them, since they are attentive with their whole heart only to those from whom they receive temporal benefits."

Holy Mother the Church taught that natives, no matter how primitive, were fully human; but in the California native the fullness of humanity seemed a rather remote potentiality. This is the judgment made in the most detailed description of the California natives written by a Franciscan missionary. And this judgment was often represented in other words. The Spanish military authorities, for instance, commonly referred to themselves, in contrast to the natives, as "the race of reason"—there was the race with reason, and the race without it.

From the standpoint of the secular authorities the missionaries were in California to make it a Spanish province, to do so by civilizing the natives. When the natives had been civilized, the mission wealth and lands would be distributed among them; the mission church itself would be turned over to the secular clergy, ordinary parish priests. The natives would become full-fledged, tax-paying citizens of the Spanish empire; the Franciscans would be sent to another frontier where they could expend their zeal for God and King.

This was the intent. And in fact in 1813 the Spanish government had ordered that all missions which had been in operation for ten years or more should be given over to the secular clergy. Although the order was impossible to implement in California—for one thing there was no secular clergy available to replace the Franciscans—the Franciscans in California thought the very idea of applying the ten year rule to their establishments was preposterous. In

California, unlike in Mexico, the natives had not even begun to apply their reason to their most immediate material needs. Only with the utmost difficulty could the California native be made to realize the superiority of the moderate, but steady, labor of cultivation to the intense, but sporadic, labor of hunting and gathering. When the salmon were running, or one of the wild fruits ripe, a friar had all he could do to keep even his most advanced neophytes from running to the hills to gorge themselves with no provision for their future.

The Franciscans did not think they should be expected to transform the native people of California into a people of reason in a mere ten years, *even if* that were the primary function of the missions. And it was *not* the primary function of the missions to transform the natives into obedient subjects of the Spanish crown.

The Franciscans were sacrificing their lives neither for personal gain nor for imperial expansion. They were sacrificing their lives to save souls that would otherwise be lost. The salvation of immortal souls, not the development of rational capacities, was their purpose for being in California; they were missionaries, not educators. The natives were taught what was needed for salvation. They were taught to cross themselves, to recite their catechisms, to be attentive and reverent during Mass, and to practice a rudimentary Christian morality. If a friar could achieve at least this with his neophytes, achieve this and also provide them with food, clothing, and shelter—if he could do all that and somehow still have energy left over, he should spend it in the attempt to bring more natives into the flock. He should seek the lost sheep rather than instruct those already of the fold in the ways of the world.

The secular authorities in California may have understood the Franciscan position regarding the natives, but they did not always sympathize with it. One governor complained, "By the Laws of the Indies the mission Indians should be free from guardianship in 10 years, with the missions becoming Indian parishes; but those of New California, at the rate they are progressing, will not become so in ten centuries; the reason, God knows, and men also know something about it."

So it is easy to see why the friars and the military authorities who had cooperated so effectively in the establishment of the mission system might be at odds over its further northward expansion. "Would there were on the go continually a company of fifty cavalrymen in this New California together with one or two missionaries who could continually visit and speak with the immense number of pagans! How many infants might be baptized, how many dying might gain eternal life!" So wrote a Franciscan friar in 1812. But the secular authorities would think the friar should improve the natives already under his control—or rather these authorities would have thought that if it had not been for the sea otter.

The otter in its way had brought California out of its isolation. Originally it had been the most remote province of the whole Spanish empire. For instance, it was a full eighteen years before a foreign vessel visited Monterey. Yet not long after this first visit it was discovered that the pelts of sea otters, one of the most plentiful of California coastal animals, could be sold in the Orient for forty dollars apiece. As a result of this discovery of the 1780s, Yankee trading vessels swarmed into California waters, like a pack of dogs. (One of the earliest was actually called *The Jackel*.)

At first the Yankees attempted to trade with the Californians for the pelts, despite the fact that Spain claimed a trade monopoly with its colony. By 1803 the Yankees had discovered a more profitable mode of operation. They would first sail to Alaska where the Russians had established their own fur gathering operation. From the Russians they would get hunting crews of native Alaskans in exchange for stores and a percentage of the take. The Yankees would then transport Aleut hunters to otter grounds in the south and supervise the slaughter.

In California these Yankee ships would stop at harbors not yet occupied by the Spanish. Near San Francisco that usually meant the bay under the protection of Point Reyes. The Aleut hunters, in their two-man kayaks, could run down sea otters, much as on land coyotes could run down rabbits. While the ship's crew sought fresh water and meat on Point Reyes, the Aleuts would work the coastal waters for otter and also seal.

In the early nineteenth century not even San Francisco Bay itself was safe from Aleutian hunting parties. The Yankees would drop their hunters on the southern Marin coast, who then would carry their kayaks across the peninsula to the bay, there to hunt.

Portions of the log of one such fur hunting ship, the *Albatross* which frequented Marin waters from 1810-12, have been preserved. When it first arrived in Drake's Bay in late November, 1810, three other Yankee ships were already there. (According to one estimate, as many as ten Yankee ships were working the California coast at one time during this period.) While working out of Drake's Bay late in 1810, the *Albatross* made an extraordinary discovery—a huge fur seal population on the Faralones, two small islands west of the entrance of the bay. The ship left a hunting party on the islands, and then continued down the California coast, hunting and, where possible, trading illegally. It was not until late 1811 that the *Albatross* returned to Drake's Bay. (This time there were two other vessels in the bay.)

In its year on the coast the *Albatross* had gorged itself on furs. It had more than six hundred sea otter pelts. And it took any pelts it could; it even had mole pelts, more than a hundred of them, in its hold. But it was the discovery of the fur seals on the Faralones that gave the *Albatross* the prospect of riches. Although the seal furs would be worth only two dollars apiece, the crew left on the Faralones for almost a year had been killing seal at a rate of close to two hundred a day. According to the log, when the *Albatross* left Drake's Bay in 1811, it carried in its hold exactly 73,402 seal furs. There were so many skins that water casks had to broken up to make room for them in the hold. The cargo was worth more than one hundred and fifty thousand dollars; the take was, in the words of the log, "very fair."

The Yankees had done well on the California coast, apparently a little too well for their own good. They had shown the Russians the profits to be made on the California coast. Soon the bear would no longer be satisfied to share the spoils of the hunt with the jackal. The very year after the *Albatross* left the California coast with its hold and even casks stuffed with furs, the Russians established their own base in California. Now if the jackal wished to cooperate with the bear, it would be the bear who would dictate the terms. By 1815 the captain of the *Albatross* had returned to his native Boston, there to live in wealthy retirement, breeding roses.

Russian occupation of northern California had been urged as early as 1806 by Count Nicolai Rezanov who had gone to San Francisco seeking relief supplies for Russia's Alaskan outpost. He sent dispatches back to Mother Russia describing the weakness of the Spanish hold on this rich California land. He imagined a Russian empire stretching from Alaska to the northern shores of San Francisco Bay. Now in 1812 Russia had begun what seemed effective action.

The site the Russians chose for Fort Ross was just to the north of Point Reyes. The establishment of this fort apparently left the Marin Peninsula as the neutral zone between the two great European powers. The Spanish, needless to say, protested what they claimed was an encroachment on their territory. The Spanish protested, and the Russian diplomats in Europe began to negotiate with them, slowly. They negotiated as the annual grain harvests from Fort Ross became greater, and the trees in the fruit orchards began to bear. Fort Ross showed promise of not only supporting itself as a hunting outpost, but also of providing supplies to Russian Alaska as well. And the Russians, like the Yankees before them, were careful not to refer to the Marin Peninsula as a part of California. For them it was a different entity entirely; it was Nova Albion.

The Spanish military leaders in San Francisco periodically sent expeditions to Fort Ross, ostensibly to hold friendly discussions, but in fact to estimate Russian progress. While negotiations continued in Europe, the Spanish military needed to dramatize the Spanish claims to the north bay region in general, and the Marin Peninsula in particular. Caesar would use Christ; the Spanish military would use the Franciscan missionaries.

So it was that Friar Sarria found himself being encouraged by Spanish authorities to extend Serra's mission procession upon the bay, to establish the first new mission in more than a decade. As Sarria looked at the sea otter which unknowingly had caused it all, he must have wondered at the ways of God with man.

The founding of Mission San Rafael was the result of a happy coincidence of interest between the secular and the religious. Such a coincidence was not as common as it once had been in California. And to understand why it was not is to understand what had happened to the California missions from the time of Serra to that of Sarria.

Perhaps it was all prophesied when a mission was finally founded in the name of Francis himself. The site for the Mission of San Francisco was found on the feast of Our Lady of Sorrows, Mary as she stood at the foot of the cross. (And hence Mission San Francisco became alternately known as Mission Dolores.) Moreover, the formal dedication for the foundation of the settlement at San Francisco took place not on the feast of Saint Francis, but on the feast of his stigmata. Our Lady of Sorrows and Saint Francis Stigmatised—none of the Franciscans who were usually so assiduous at seeing divine signs even noticed this coincidence. Had they noticed, they would have had a dark glimpse of the future both of this mission and of the whole Franciscan effort in California. The mission procession in California was not to be a procession of triumph; rather it was a procession to a crucifixion. California, Queen California, would offer the sons of Francis not even a quick martyrdom, but only the slow agony of the cross.

The divisions within California were deeper than a simple difference in policy between the mission authorities and the secular government. The friars, for instance, believed that their very work as priests was being undermined by the Spanish soldiers. The friars would make more spiritual progress with the natives were it not for the obvious material corruption of the military.

The soldiers were, the friars had to admit, necessary for defense, defense against grizzlies, defense against aggressive gentiles (as the pagan natives were called), defense against potential foreign invasion. The California natives certainly should not fall into the hands of the schismatic Russians or the heretical Yankees. But was it any worse that they fall into the hands of immoral Spaniards?

The natives, like children of original sin everywhere, were sexually lax. It was only with the greatest of difficulty that they were made to understand the requirements of Christian morality in this sphere. And certainly fornication was not the worst of their sins in the state of nature. Did not the women, to remain comely, endeavor to abort their children—and, failing that, sometimes even strangle them at birth? With such a people the regulation of sexual activity would be difficult even in the best of circumstances. Did not the young unmarried women have to be literally locked in their sleeping quarters at night?

Yet these same natives—yes, even married women and young boys—were not safe around the very soldiers who had been sent to California to protect them. These Spanish laymen, these people of reason, who should provide examples of Christian virtue, rather, as often as not, offer instruction in Christian depravation. How are these poor natives, these children whose minds are so weak, to comprehend the contradiction between the teaching of the friars and the practice of the soldiers? Some of the California Franciscans must have known of the prayer attributed to one of their predecessors in the North American missions, Friar Magril, who implored the Deity: "A militibus, libera nos Domine." From the military, deliver us, O Lord.

And it was not only the immorality of the soldiers against which the Franciscans continually complained; it was also their indolence. Assignment to California was perhaps the least desirable in all of New Spain. Often it came as the result of failure or malfeasance in another place, much as Galvez had punished soldiers who had mismanaged the affairs of Baja California by sending them on the Sacred Expedition. So the ordinary soldiers stationed in California might, without too much exaggeration, be considered the dregs of the Spanish overseas military. Nonetheless, they had their pride. They were, after all, descended, more or less, from the noble conquistadors. And they were here, at this God-forsaken, friar-infested outpost, to defend the honor of the Spanish Empire, if need be with their lives. Therefore, they should be treated with the respect due warriors. Since they might have to fight, they should not have to work.

All the foreign visitors agreed: they did not work. Phrases like "congenital idleness" and "natural repugnance for work" are commonplace in foreign accounts of the California conquistadors.

What particularly exasperated the friars was not just that the soldiers were practicing the very indolence and immorality from which the missions were trying to wean the natives, but also that the missions were expected to support the military in their relative comfort. As one friar put it, "The Indians go barefoot in order that they might provide shoes for the troops and their families; they eat their food without butter that the troops may have it; they do not taste beans in order to be able to deliver them to the military store."

This was written in 1816, the year before the founding of San Rafael. If it had been written only five years earlier, it would have been so overstated as to be mere polemic (a genre the friars sometimes employed when complaining against the military). At the turn of the century neophytes were expected to work at times around the fort, and the friars were expected to provide a certain amount of material support at reduced rates; but this was nothing that would place any strain on the missions (if the soldiers only would behave like Christians).

However, by 1811 Mexico was moving toward independence from Spain, with all the attendant social disruption. For California this meant a virtual end to material support from Mexico and Spain.

The supply ships could not be counted upon to arrive at their regularly scheduled intervals. When they did arrive, they would usually not have the money owed the military in salaries and the like; neither would they have money from the Pious Fund for the missionaries.

One Yankee trader who arrived in San Francisco during this period seeking illegal trading privileges professed only the highest of motives. He wished only, at a small profit, to clothe the nakedness of the soldiers. He did not get his trade concessions (even after he proposed marriage to the commandante's aging daughter), but his observation about the soldiers was accurate enough. The California military was becoming a collective charity case, one that placed them at the mercy of the Franciscans.

A Franciscan might find the role of mendicant in tatters an enobling experience; but a self-styled follower of Cortes would respond differently. And the mercy of the California Franciscans did not descend upon the military like the gentle rain from heaven; it came heavy with protests and scolding.

Not surprisingly, tales began to be told in the forts about the immense, secret wealth of the missions. Eyewitnesses, or those who had heard them, would tell of friars boarding ships back to Mexico, friars with habits so heavy with hidden gold they could barely waddle. So the missions became in the imaginations of much of the soldiery the local equivalent of the seven golden cities—but these "cities" the soldiers by their honor as Spaniards could not plunder, except in their dreams.

Of course, the soldiers and the settlers which the government was now deporting to California did not have to look for secret stashes of precious metals to find mission wealth. It was there before their eyes—thousands of acres of good land, well-tilled fields, and orchards, and gardens, huge herds of cattle and sheep, more horses than could be used, and hundreds of natives to do your bidding. That was a wealth far beyond that which any soldier or settler forced to California could ever expect to possess, even in a fraction.

Nonetheless, for the Franciscans it was a cross. At about the time San Rafael was founded, Franciscans were actually negotiating to give the missions to another order. Sarria polled his fellow friars, and they were unanimous in their wish to leave, especially the northern missions. (The transfer did not occur, only because the Spanish government tried to place too many restrictions on the new order.)

One of the missionaries was not just speaking for himself when he wrote: "There are difficulties all around, and I am overburdened with cares which render life wearisome. There is hardly any of the religious in me, and I scarcely know what to do in these troublesome times. I made the vows of Friar Minor; instead I must manage temporalities, sow grain, raise sheep, horses, and cows, preach, baptize, bury the dead, visit the sick, direct carts, haul stone, lime, etc. These things are as disagreeable as thorns, bitter, hard, unbearable, and they rob me of time, tranquility, and health, both of soul and body."

The Franciscans were weary. There were increasing reports of chronic headaches and melancholy. Missionaries now regularly requested, as was their right, to be relieved after ten years in the field; but usually they had to stay simply because no one could be found willing to take their places in Serra's vineyard.

Yet these were Franciscans, men who sought out hardship for God's sake. And they were the best of the Franciscans, those willing to endure most for Christ's sake. As a group, they were not the kind of men who were easily wearied, men who turned from difficulty. The threats of foreign invasion, the growing indifference of the central government, the immorality and the indolence of the military, the backwardness of the natives, the grizzlies, the fogs, the loneliness—all this, by itself, would not have been enough to discourage these men as a group. But there was more.

In the early nineteenth century the Mexican government planned to establish a colony of convicts at the very border of one of the missions. The Father President, needless to say, wrote an eloquent protest of this decision, one of the many he would write during his tenure. Government regulations explicitly forbade the establishment of any colonies so close to a mission, to say nothing of one composed of convicts.

That the authorities in Mexico would wish to do so, that the Franciscans would protest, that the protest would be denied—all this was to be expected. What was interesting about this incident was the explanation the Mexican officials offered for rejecting the protest. The officials, in fact, conceded the central point of the Franciscan protest. Government regulations were quite explicit. The proposed colony was in violation of these regulations, at least of their letter. However, the spirit should also be considered. The regulations were made to protect the mission natives. Hence the colony did not violate the spirit of the regulations. The mission natives did not require any such protection. The natives needed no such protection because they were, as everybody knew, *dying out.*

The natives, the mission natives were dying out. It could not be denied; the pattern was now clear. Baja California had already become depopulated, and the natives were well on their way toward extinction. Now they were dying in upper California as well, in increasingly large numbers. Northern California, from Monterey up, was, if anything, worse than the south.

The friars had given up everything to care for this people of California, to die for them if need be, to be martyred by their hand if God so willed. And the friars had cared for them as best they could. They had fed them, clothed them, taught them, and, most important, they had saved many souls. They had come to this remote place as instruments of God, instruments of the light, of life everlasting.

And yet the natives were dying. And the Franciscans in their zeal had been, however unwittingly, the instruments of their physical death. The friars had willed it no more than the sea otters had willed the coming of the Russians. Even so, the friars had brought with them the soldiers, and after them the settlers. And these had carried with them diseases, especially *gallico,* the French disease, syphilis.

The natives could not be blamed. They were children of nature, children of a fallen nature. And the soldiers, were even the soldiers to blame? Surely some would be damned for what they had done, but many would be forgiven, saved by the wounds of Christ. The soldiers too were children of Adam and Eve, unable to perceive the horrible consequences of their acts.

But the consequences were horrible. By 1800 syphilis had become almost universal among the mission natives. Perhaps the friars might have had some chance if they could have begun anew with each generation of natives, to teach once again the value of chastity and the consequences of incontinence. But they could not. Syphilis had become, as one friar put it, "a baby's only birthright."

At one mission—Purissima Conception, The Immaculate Conception—women had ceased to give birth to living babies. This was where Friar Gil had been stationed before becoming the first missionary at San Rafael. While at Purissima Conception, Gil had become adept at performing caesarian sections. That procedure, whatever risk it held for the mother, preserved a chance that the syphilitic baby might be removed from the womb and baptized before it died. Father Sarria had recommended that other California missionaries learn and follow Friar Gil's methods.

As for Gil himself, he began to suffer from a heart condition. In 1816 he had requested to be sent home from California. Instead, he was offered the new mission at San Rafael. To have a new mission among gentile natives, even to have the possibility of a quick martyrdom, must have seemed preferable to the slow agony of Purissima Conception. Nonetheless, Gil seems to have been assigned to the new mission because of his medical reputation. San Rafael was to be, at least in part, a medical mission. It was to help relieve the suffering of natives at the San Francisco mission.

San Francisco was by reputation the least healthy of the missions. (Rumor had it that syphilis was introduced into upper California by the first group of settlers who arrived at San Francisco.) Not only were the natives as badly infected with syphilis as elsewhere, but also the cold fogs and sandstorms of the barren San Francisco Peninsula made them particularly susceptible to other diseases.

One unspecified disease killed a substantial proportion of the neophytes in 1795; as a result, many of the survivors ran away, and could only be coaxed back with considerable difficulty. In the midst of this, one of the Franciscans became insane. (The other friars said he had suffered a blow to the head.) He charged the friars with plotting against him, withholding food from the natives, beating them. It was their fault the natives ran away, not his. Eventually he had to be sent back to Mexico; on the same ship was a friar from another mission who had gone insane after only one month in the field.

The San Francisco mission was losing an estimated thirty to forty per cent of its population to disease each year. None of the missions in the early nineteenth century could maintain their population without recruiting from an ever widening area; but this was especially true of San Francisco. So it was that in the early nineteenth century Marin names began to appear regularly, and in significant numbers, in the San Francisco baptismal records. Yet the death rate continued to be high. And the periodic epidemics became increasingly deadly. In 1808, a measles epidemic killed almost all the children under ten, and many of the parents. Virtually all the neophytes ran away this time.

The problem of recruiting new converts, and of retrieving runaways, became increasingly severe. The temptation to use force was great. And the gentiles of Marin and the east side of the bay were now understandably hostile to the Spanish presence. Mission San Jose, which had been established on the southeast corner of the bay, was in almost constant danger. Pitched battles were fought between the Spanish and the natives on the east bay shore. When the friars of San Francisco sent a group of fourteen unarmed neophytes to the north bay to persuade some runaways to return, they were attacked and seven were killed.

And so, with a Russian presence in the north and potential native allies on the peninsula itself, the decision was made that a mission should be established in Marin with a friar who was willing "to shed my blood if necessary." The mission was consecrated to San Rafael, the archangel of healing. San Rafael was an apt choice.

The land around the bay of Saint Francis was suffering many hostile divisions, between Spanish and Russian, between friar and soldier, between neophyte and gentile. They were so many wounds that needed healing; and like the running sores of the syphilitic their healing would require an angelic intervention.

But the intervention was not to come. The natives were dying, and the missions with them. And there was no one for the Franciscans to blame, except each himself for some sin he did not know or thought long forgiven. No one to blame except Him whom they could not blame. And the cup would not pass from them.

The history of Mission San Rafael Archangel in its first decade was a throw-back to earlier, simpler times of the California missions, the happy times. It was as if the age of Serra had come again in one small place. Mission San Rafael was a new day, late in the year.

The number of neophytes steadily grew. In 1820 there were 590 neophytes; by 1828 there were 1,140. In the mid-twenties the population at San Rafael had surpassed that of San Francisco, and San Rafael became an autonomous mission. Throughout its first decade and longer, San Rafael was mercifully spared the epidemics which had ravaged San Francisco. Syphilis must have been present. (It was observed to be widespread among the gentile tribes to the north by the mid-thirties.) Nonetheless, it seems to have been contained. San Rafael had one of the lowest death rates of any mission in the system.

As the population grew, so did the neophyte-cared-for food

supply. A large orchard and vineyard was established a short distance to the southwest of the mission. Nearby must have been the
extensive vegetable garden; a little further away the large fields of
grains. In an average year during the 1820s San Rafael produced
2,400 bushels of grain, about half of that wheat. Across the ridge
which protected the mission to the north were the plains on which
the mission herds grazed; by 1830 they had grown to 1,500 head of
beef, 1,800 sheep, and 450 horses.

The prosperity of San Rafael was reflected in its almost continuous building. First built, of course, was the mission proper. This
was originally a long building—roughly 80' x 40' x 16'—which was
divided by partitions into a chapel, sacristy, priest's room, dining
room, kitchen, and guest room; the attic area of the building serving
as a granary. By 1820 there had been no less than four additions to
the basic mission building.

Still no provision for neophyte residence had been made; the
neophytes were expected to live in their tule huts about the mission
grounds. In the 1820s, however, this changed. The population had
grown so large that permanent structures were required. Between
1820 and 1826 perhaps as many as nine such buildings were added
to the mission complex. Some of these, such as the separate house
for single women, were not particularly notable. But the five or six
structures which were the main living areas for the bulk of the population were said to be the most impressive structures of the whole
compound. These large buildings were two stories, the upper story
of each a dormitory housing perhaps more than one hundred, the
lower story a series of workshops.

By the late 1820s the major construction was finished. A new
separate church had been finished as well as separate residences for
the military, a tannery, woodsheds, and an aqueduct to the spring
that supplied the mission with water. The orchard and vineyard had
been enclosed in walls, as had the cemetery.

Almost all the basic building was done with adobe. The first
mission building had an adjacent corridor roofed by tules, as if a
token of the old ways. But tule houses were to be a thing of the past.
Suitable soil was wetted and mixed with straw; the prepared mud
poured into wooden molds, usually approximately 4" x 12" x 24"
in size. The adobe brick was then cured in the sun. The tiles that
would roof the permanent structures were somewhat more compli-
cated to make; they had to be fired in a kiln.

The adobe, unlike the tiles, needed continual tending, lest it crumble back into its earthen state. Indeed, the descriptions of the constant care the neophytes had to exercise on the mission adobe does not lack parallels with the descriptions of the constant care that the missionaries had to exercise on the neophytes, lest they too crumble back into their natural state.

This tendency the Franciscans attempted to overcome by regimen, by routine. The neophyte who tended the adobe tended also his own soul. Everyone was to have his task; old women could gather kindling, small children could scare the birds away from the orchard. And everyone's life was to be regulated by the church's bell.

At sunrise they would be awakened by the bell, so they could meet in the church for morning prayers. Shortly after prayers another ringing of the bell would proclaim that breakfast was ready. At the next bell all went to work, some in the shops, some in the fields, some in the gardens, some with the herds, each at his appointed task. The bells would signal lunch, the return to work, evening prayer, dinner, the end of the day. Those needing instruction in their catechism would have special times for it immediately after breakfast and lunch.

This was the daily rhythm of time established on the Marin Peninsula decades after it had been established elsewhere in California. By establishing this daily rhythm, and by enriching it with the weekly sabbath and the annual sacred feasts and holy seasons, the friars hoped to tend their flock to eternal life in spite of a natural world governed by corruption and decay.

Of course, there would be some neophytes who would succumb to the temptations of the old ways. A single friar and a few soldiers could not closely supervise the more than a thousand neophytes. To slip away would not be difficult. When such occurred, the missionary would be faced with the decision of whether or not to try to persuade or even to force the runaway to return. If the native had been baptized, then the Franciscan had the legal rights that a father had over a minor child—the legal rights and the moral responsibilities.

According to custom, runaways and other offenders against the regular life of the mission were not usually punished for the first offence. Repetitions, however, could lead to time in the stocks, or even a lashing. The friars, who if they followed the example of Serra would flagellate themselves for their own sins, could not have been squeamish about physical punishment as such, although they always had others administer it. And it is known that repeated runaways, who must have been a particular problem in unhealthy missions, were shackled. There are no reports of such extreme measures having been taken at San Rafael, any more than there are such reports in the early days of the mission system.

The Franciscan who had the good providence to be at San Rafael during its blossoming into a full mission was not Friar Gil. His heart condition worsened, and in 1819 he was transferred to another mission where the other friars could care for him should he have another attack. The friar blest with the assignment to San Rafael was Juan Amoros.

Amoros, by all accounts, deserved his good providence. Amoros was a true Franciscan. He was not an impressive man in appearance; he was small, dark, his face pockmarked. No one ever commented on his powers as a preacher, or a theologian, or even a conversationalist. Yet even settlers who ordinarily only spoke of the friars to slander them, spoke of his virtue.

Amoros, unlike many of his fellow Franciscans, seems to have adjusted well to the changing state of the missions. He took a conciliatory attitude toward the military and settlers. At San Carlos, where he was first assigned, he would say Mass for them and teach their children catechism. (Some of these children, when adults, would remember the treasure Friar Amoros would have hidden in his habit for those who had learned their lesson well—dried fruit.) His tolerant attitude extended even beyond the Spanish people of reason. He spoke out in favor of open trade with foreign vessels. The Yankee Protestants were, he suggested, also "children of God."

In regards to the various chores required in running a mission Amoros was equally open-hearted. At San Carlos he did the annual accounting. One can still see the originals of his sums, with "Viva Jesus" written across the top of each page. He seems to have taken intrinsic pleasure in mechanical objects. Story has it he built a waterclock at San Rafael which still was keeping good time decades after his death. He, a born teacher of childish minds, could instruct his Marin converts in the rudiments of their new faith, and in the mechanics of a civilized life; and at the same time he could be expected to remain on friendly terms with the military who would guard his outpost, and with the Russians who were threatening it from the north. All of which he did, and thereby San Rafael prospered.

Although he missed the worst of it, Amoros did suffer some of the vexations that were making life unbearable for other missionaries. The Russians at Fort Ross were a source of worry; but even this was not as bad as could have reasonably been expected. By the 1820s Fort Ross itself was struggling. The furs had been too heavily hunted by the Yankees; and one leader of Ross would claim in the 1830s, with some exaggeration, that the otter was virtually extinct along the northern California coast. (This would be so only after they had been systematically hunted by rifle.) Decisive action or slow decay seemed the choice which faced the Russian empire regarding its California colony; the bear seemed incapable of decisive actions, and so slow decay it was. Nonetheless, this decay indirectly brought its own trouble for Amoros and Mission San Rafael.

Given the weakening Russian presence, the San Francisco military authorities wished to press their advantage by placing a mission to the north of San Rafael, almost directly to the west of Fort Ross, in the Sonoma Valley. Such an establishment would effectively cut off Russian access to even the northern tip of San Francisco Bay, much as San Rafael had cut off access to its entrance.

To implement this plan the secular authorities used divisions within the Franciscan order itself. They found a young friar, Father Altimira, who was so impatient with the conditions at San Francisco that he was willing to establish, on his individual religious authority and with the support of the secular authorities, his own mission.

Without consulting his religious superiors, he went ahead with his plans and established what he called New San Francisco in the area east of Fort Ross. In presenting his superiors with his *fait accompli* he suggested that the success of his venture would be assured if Old San Francisco and San Rafael were closed and their neophytes transferred to his better-situated establishment. Thus, for a time Amoros was faced with the possibility that his thriving mission would be destroyed in a conflict of wills between the military and religious authorities. All of the assets of San Rafael had been inventoried in preparation for the transfer before a compromise was finally reached which allowed all three missions to continue.

This crisis was scarcely passed before another one threatened the whole Franciscan presence in California. In 1821 Mexico had become independent from Spain; this made the Spanish missionaries aliens in the Mexican province of California. A law was passed which required the Franciscans to swear allegiance to a new Mexican constitution, a constitution which the Franciscans regarded as anti-clerical. Father Altimira, always impetuous in defense of his right to missionary activity, simply fled the country.

Amoros, like Sarria, attempted to take the middle, conciliatory path. He would not swear the oath, as did some of the older and infirm friars. Nor would he defy it. Rather he simply promised to obey any legal civil authority that did not require him to go against his conscience. For a time it looked as if he, and the others who refused to swear allegiance, would be deported. But the old problem remained of finding priests willing to take their place. They were permitted to stay, and San Rafael continued to flourish.

While it flourished Mission San Rafael Archangel had but one foreign visitor who left any detailed description. He was a touring Russian, Otto von Kotzebue, who stopped at San Rafael in the 1820s on his way from San Francisco to Fort Ross.

Kotzebue was accompanied from San Francisco by a Spanish settler, a Don Estudillo who looked to Kotzebue like a figure out of Cervantes. Kotzebue described him as "in old Spanish costume, with a heavy sword, still heavier spurs, a dagger and pistols in his belt, and a staff in his hand." Estudillo did not weaken this impression when on the boat trip across the bay he began to boast of his learning. He was, he said, far better educated than most Spaniards in California; he had read, besides *Don Quixote*, no less than four books.

Perhaps at this point Kotzebue teased Estudillo about the friars, all of whom presumably had read at least six, even seven books. Estudillo, whatever the reason, began a diatribe against the whole mission system. And so Kotzebue heard what he had likely heard elsewhere in California. No native ever presented himself freely to the missionaries. The friars send out dragoons who lasso the gentiles and drag them back to the missions half-dead. The friars did not care about the sincerity of the conversions. They were, according to Estudillo, "solely intent on their private gain." They "enrich themselves here by the severe labor imposed on their converts, and then return to Spain with their treasures."

Kotzebue was pleased to hear all this, not necessarily because he believed it, but because it revealed the deep division that existed within California. It showed that the Mexican hold on northern

California was very weak. Kotzebue wrote: "I confess I could not help speculating upon the benefits this country would derive from becoming a province of our powerful empire, and how useful it would prove to possess."

It was with such aggressive thoughts on his mind that the Russian got his first glimpse of Mission San Rafael. This perhaps helps explain a mistake he then made. He mistook the name of the mission. Instead of the archangel of bodily healing he thought it was the archangel of military victory. Kotzebue thought he saw not San Rafael, but San Gabriel.

As the boat moved closer to the estuary where it would land, Kotzebue was struck by the beauty of the place. "The mission of San Gabriel peeped from among the foliage of its ancient oaks. Many horses belonging to the mission were grazing in a beautiful meadow by the waterside, in perfect harmony with a herd of small deer, which are very numerous in this country. The locality of this mission . . . is still better chosen than that of the celebrated Santa Clara."

Nonetheless, the beauty of the mission had its ominous side. The same ridge which sheltered the mission also served as a hiding place for hostile gentiles "who have already once succeeded in burning the buildings of the mission, and still keep the friars continually on the watch against similar depradations."

Like most of his account, this part was not without factual mistakes. There were not "friars," but only one friar at San Rafael, Juan Amoros. Nonetheless, he was correct about the attack that had been mounted against the mission by the gentiles.

Kotzebue was undoubtedly reporting accurately when he wrote that this Marin mission had "much more the appearance of a defensive outpost than do the other missions." He might himself take lightly the reports of the bravery of the gentiles, probably because he used Don Estudillo as a measure of what Californians regarded as bravery; but he could not deny that the precautions taken by the troops at San Rafael were more than quixotic bluster.

"The garrison, six men strong, is always ready for service on the slightest alarm. Having been driven from my bed during the night by vermin, I saw two sentinels, fully armed, keeping guard towards the mountain, each of them beside a large fire; every two minutes they rang a bell which was hung between two pillars and were regularly answered by the yipping of the coyote."

Kotzebue was seeing the results of one final crisis which Mission

San Rafael had to survive in its first decade, a major gentile attack. In 1824-25 there was general unrest among the Indian population of California; attacks on the missions became widespread and frequent. And on the Marin Peninsula there might have been specific cause for hostility. After the Altimira and citizenship difficulties, some of the largest buildings were erected at the mission. The two-story neophyte buildings, for instance, are first mentioned in a report of 1826. It was as if Amoros wished to give visible evidence that his mission was a permanent thing. This evidence of permanence might have impressed eyes other than those for which it was intended.

The actual details of the attack are garbled, and inconsistent on important details. Nonetheless, there are a few details common to all accounts. The mission seems to have been taken by surprise, and almost overwhelmed. And the ultimate objective of the attack seems to have been the death of Juan Amoros himself. He was lucky to have escaped with his life.

According to one version he was saved only by the action of the neophytes themselves. They formed a human shield around him, to preserve him from blows or arrows. In this manner they got him to the bay shore, and placed him afloat alone on the bay in a tule boat. (Another version has him put on the boat with a mother and child.) And so, while the gentile attack was being desperately repulsed at the mission, Juan Amoros was being providentially drifted by bay currents across to San Francisco and safety.

IV
Marin's Peninsula

Juan Amoros died in July, 1832. Nothing memorable was recorded concerning his death, except the opinion of the friar who attended him that this man was a saint. The premature deaths of Amoros and another California friar were used by the president of the missions as the occasion for a bitter denunciation of the secular authorities.

But very few were trembling before Father President's words these days, no matter how bitter he made them. Friar Amoros, fortunate in his assignment to San Rafael, was fortunate also in the time of his death. 1832 marked the date of the first recorded major epidemic to pass through the Marin Peninsula. And, as Father President must have anticipated, not long thereafter the secularization of the missions began.

In 1840 one California friar wrote: "All is destruction, all is misery, humiliation, and despair. Only six years have sufficed not only to annihilate the missions but also to destroy in us every hope of restoring these establishments, reared at the cost of so much toil and sacrifice." Although Amoros was spared all this, others were not.

There survives a glimpse of Mission San Rafael after secularization. The date of the record is 1844. A man named Pierce wrote of coming to Marin to inspect a ranch that was for sale at the north of the peninsula. After crossing the bay, Pierce stayed with John Reed, himself the first settler on the peninsula. Reed had come to Marin in the early 1830s. He had first tried to establish himself north of Mission San Rafael. Amoros had advised against the decision, because he thought the natives there were still too hostile to tolerate a permanent European presence. Reed ignored the advice, to his sorrow. The natives ran off all his stock, and he had to flee to Mission

San Rafael for protection. The friar, in his usual generous spirit, allowed Reed to replace his livestock from mission herds. Reed then successfully established himself in southern Marin.

It was Reed who guided Pierce toward his prospective ranch. On their way they stopped at San Rafael, or, rather, the ruins of San Rafael. Pierce himself was not surprised by the delapidated condition of the mission; he had already concluded that secularization had "been nothing but a course of plunder and rapine—all the missions in California have been almost entirely despoiled of their property."

Reed, of course, knew this far better than Pierce. He also knew the friar who eventually succeeded Amoros and now lived amidst these ruins. Reed had already settled in Marin when Friar Quijas had arrived from Mexico, proud of his Indian heritage and ready to serve the secularized missions, both San Rafael and San Francisco Solano, which had been assigned to his care. He knew of Quijas' facility with native tongues, and his eloquence at the pulpit. Reed must have heard how courageously Quijas had attempted to defend the neophytes at San Francisco Solano from the encroachments of the most powerful settlers. He would have known how Quijas protested to the authorities about the pillaging of the mission, the seduction of its women, the treatment of the men as serfs. Quijas had protested, removed himself to San Rafael, and waited for the malefactors to get their due. But that had all happened years ago, and Reed also knew the friar as he was now, now that he no longer waited. Reed himself had for a time been the secular administrator of the mission. He had seen the decline of Quijas into a ruin of what he had once been. He knew that Quijas had taken to drink and now no longer kept his vows.

Reed knew all that, but Reed also knew how to get along in a land like this. He did not burden a prospective neighbor with the sordid details of local gossip. About San Rafael he only mentioned the one thing that had not changed since Kotzebue's visit. The vermin that had awakened the Russian were apparently still there, or at least their descendants were. Reed told Pierce that San Rafael was "famous for its fleas."

Reed and Pierce had stopped at San Rafael because a storm threatened. Rather than risk getting caught in it, they turned back, and returned to Reed's ranch. If Reed hoped he could spare Pierce the facts about Friar Quijas until after he had decided on the ranch, the unexpected return to the Reed ranch made that impossible. Reed might decline to talk about Quijas. But the friar was there to greet their return, drunk.

Worse still, Reed's wife was nowhere to be seen. Reed eventually found her hiding in the woods near their house. These woods were frequented by bears, but Reed's wife had preferred to risk them than to remain alone in the house with Quijas whose behavior toward her had been inappropriate.

Pierce thought he understood what had happened, but he could not understand Reed's response. He thought Reed must have feared the priest, or rather feared some law which made striking a priest a capital offense. Why else would Reed be so kindly to such a despicable person?

Reed simply told the priest of his wife's accusations, and then listened while the priest began "to rave like a madman." People did not give him the proper respect; if he were only a soldier, then they would respect him. Quijas suddenly pulled a knife from within his habit, and thrust it at Reed who only stepped aside and did nothing in reprisal. Quijas, with the knife still in his hand, seemed to be calmed by his ineffectual attempt at violence. Eventually he gave the knife to Reed, and began to weep. He implored Reed to stab him in the heart. He said that "it was his punishment and he deserved it."

Pierce never did buy the ranch. When he finally saw it, it did not suit him.

Between Juan Amoros and Jose Quijas, Mission San Rafael had been briefly under the charge of three different Franciscans. Of the three, only the brief tenure of Rafael Moreno was notable. Moreno, if one is to believe remarks he made much later, was convinced that the native Californians were as capable of civilization as any of the self-styled race of reason. It was not their mental capacities but the pernicious influence of the village traditions that held them back. They had simply to be removed to the healthier, less superstitious environment of the mission. If, however, the natives were left in their villages, they would never be able to compete with the Europeans. They would be fated to extinction.

Possibly Moreno was acting on this conviction when as missionary at San Rafael he occasioned the hostility of some gentile tribes in the north of the peninsula. A battle was fought, and a number of gentiles killed. As a result, Moreno was removed from his position, pending an investigation by his Franciscan superiors. Although he was eventually exonerated, he was never allowed to return to Marin, or ever again to head his own mission.

What is interesting is that Moreno was removed for exciting the hostility of a gentile tribe. What earlier might have been regarded as at most imprudent or overzealous, was now treated as possibly criminal.

The reason for this is simple enough. That particular gentile tribe was an ally of Mexican California, an ally sworn to the defense of its northern frontier against all enemies, whether European or native. This tribe was more important to the security of California than any missionary.

European alliances with gentile tribes, as much as the secularization of the missions, represented an important change in the life of the Indians. Just as the neophytes could now inherit the mission wealth, and become free citizens in the Mexican province of California, so gentile tribes could retain their internal autonomy by allying themselves with the Europeans against hostile tribes. As the neophytes could now have both Christianity and freedom from priestly domination, so the gentiles could reject Christianity and still benefit from European arms.

The new frame of things was, in short, apparently in the interest of the Indians, both Christian and gentile alike. This appearance, however, was misleading. Alliances with gentile tribes no less than secularization of the missions were instruments to take from the natives what freedom and wealth they had. The neophytes would be given some of the mission wealth they and the Franciscans had accumulated, but only so that all this wealth could eventually find its way into the hands of people of reason. The gentile tribes would be given autonomy to fight other gentile tribes, but only until these were vanquished; then their tribal autonomy would no longer be useful for the people of reason who would have gained control of virtually all the newly pacified land. The natives, both Christian and gentile alike, would be left landless and powerless. Their freedom would consist in choosing to live as a virtual serf on the new European ranches which would now divide Marin, or to live as a vagrant on the fringes of these ranches.

And this is what happened throughout the mission area of California. But on the Marin Peninsula and in the rest of the mission region north of the bay it was achieved with remarkable efficiency. The Marin natives, for instance, were reduced to this state in less than ten years after the secularization of San Rafael. The reason for this efficiency was that the north bay region had become the fief of probably the ablest of the people of reason, Mariano Vallejo.

Vallejo was one of the new generation of native Californians of European blood. His father had been a captain at Monterey. Mariano had been given his first communion and taught his catechism by Juan Amoros. And his education did not end with his catechism. Vallejo managed to read widely in the pagan classics. Eventually Mariano would name one of his own sons Plato. Yet it was not the soft contemplative reason of the Greeks that Vallejo most admired, but rather the hard pragmatic reason of the Romans. History, not philosophy, taught the highest form of reason, and its token was not the possession of truth but the possession of power.

When Vallejo and his contemporaries achieved the secularization of the missions, Mariano chose for his own sphere of action the north bay region. He was the military commander on this frontier, and here, near Mission San Francisco Solano, he chose to establish his own ranch and fort.

To some this might have seemed a strange choice, with less troublesome land at hand. But whoever questioned his choice had obviously not read Roman history. The basis for all power was military strength. Vallejo, living on the northern frontier, would be justified, even after he resigned from the military, in behaving like a commander. In any dispute with the central authority he would have battle-seasoned troops at hand, much as would a Roman commander of the northern German legions.

A story Vallejo liked to tell shows this. During the 1840s there was a particularly irascible Mexican governor of California; in fact, Governor Chico was so irascible that the people of Monterey had come to call him simply, "The Bear." Chico had at one point ordered Vallejo to Monterey because he had exceeded his authority. (Vallejo was accustomed to acting as if entirely autonomous.) Vallejo's friends in Monterey, who were also Chico's enemies, feared that Mariano was about to lose his freedom. They had, however, underestimated Vallejo's resources.

Vallejo arrived in Monterey accompanied by a bodyguard of his most ferocious-looking native troops which likely included his most prized warrior, the 6'7" chieftain called by the Europeans

Solano, but known to his own people as Stone Hands. Even The Bear was cowed. When they were alone, Chico meekly asked if Vallejo really lived amidst such people. Yes, Vallejo replied, he really did. How did he survive? He simply followed the Roman policy of divide and conquer. Instead of being arrested for insubordination, Vallejo found himself being publically praised by his governor for his great service to the California commonwealth. Then his Monterey friends privately feted him as "the tamer of the wild beast."

Vallejo perceived himself as a tamer of wild beasts. By placing himself between the Mexicans and the savages he gained a measure of control over both. But it was his control over the savages on which Vallejo most prided himself. Indeed, he regarded the European occupation of California as a feat of barbarian-taming comparable to that of the Romans of old.

Mariano Vallejo not only sought historical precedents for the European achievement in California, he hoped it would stand as a historical precedent for future generations. The Europeans had achieved in California something worth immortalizing, a monument not to their brute strength, but to their intelligence. And Vallejo, himself so prominent in the California achievement, wished also to be its historian.

In the 1830s Mariano Vallejo had already begun to collect documents and to write his history of California. His first version of the history was destroyed in a fire, but this did not deter him. The story was too important to be left untold, untold by someone of Vallejo's clear-minded perspective. Late in life, Vallejo completed a second version. His history of California, needless to say, is in marked contrast to Franciscan sources.

The history of California was for Vallejo essentially a history of conquest. It is the story of how a small, greatly out-numbered group of Europeans managed to gain control over a vast land. They had achieved this because they were a people of reason, a people who could effectively exploit the divisions which existed among the natives.

Franciscan sources continually bemoan the tribal divisions which they found among the natives. Only with great difficulty could the missionaries get neophytes to associate with converts from other tribes with which a tradition of hostility had existed. But for Vallejo these traditional hatreds were a precious natural resource. They permitted the Europeans to follow more easily what he called in his history "the Roman policy of divide and conquer." If there had not already been these divisions, the Europeans would have had to create them.

As for the Franciscans, Vallejo presents them simply as the unwitting propaganda arm of the military. The native Californians were a noble people who had the misfortune to live in a priest-ridden society. Vallejo attributes most of the immorality of the native Californians to the influence of their priests. The Europeans, shrewdly realizing that they did not have the military force simply to take California from its hundreds of thousands of inhabitants, exploited the natives' weakness for priests. The sincere and zealous Franciscans, under the protection of the military, would seek converts, natives willing to transfer their superstitious loyalty from native priests to European priests. This tactic enabled the Europeans to gain a foothold along the California coast with tens of thousands of the natives professing loyalty to the Europeans. But the tactic also allowed the clergy to usurp temporarily the position of leadership that was naturally the military's. Franciscans wanted the European advance to be essentially religious. In particular, they wished to reduce the military to guardians of mission interests.

In short, the clergy eventually became an impediment to the further conquest of California. Vallejo wished his readers to recognize that any extension of European control over California after 1800 was due to the initiative of the military. For instance, the establishment of Mission San Rafael was given little space in Vallejo's history. Rather, he wished to discuss at length the military operations which made this establishment possible.

Until 1817 a gentile chief of the Marin Peninsula had effectively prevented any European settlement in the area. He and his band would attack any Europeans found there. However, in 1817 in an attack on a military party returning from an exploratory expedition he was captured, and placed in the fort at San Francisco.

Although a mission could then be established, the north bay region was still not safe. To the northeast of the Marin Peninsula there was a particularly bellicose tribe, feared on the peninsula and capable of making difficulties for Europeans there. This tribe was sought-out by a Lieutenant Rafael Garcia in 1818. The fighting lasted more than two days, and Garcia himself admitted that only the superior weapons of the Europeans enabled them finally to prevail. The natives retreated to their village, which was surrounded by the

Spaniards. Then the chief, realizing his defeat was complete, ordered the whole village with warriors, women, and children still in it burnt to the ground.

In his account of this incident Vallejo only quoted Garcia's report verbatim. He did not mention that Garcia, because of this incident, was accused of murder by the missionaries who said he ordered the fire himself.

Vallejo did think that Garcia had been too aggressive. The destruction of this particular native tribe might have worked out well, thanks to European firearms. However, this would not provide a model for European conquest of all California. In an isolated battle the Europeans had greater forces, but in the long run this was dwarfed by the mere numbers of natives. Europeans had to use their reason to set the natives against each other. Divide and conquer— Mariano Vallejo never tired of repeating his one Latin lesson.

Mariano Vallejo believed that whatever Rafael Garcia's excesses in the north bay, he had at least perceived the conquest correctly—that is, in military terms. As much could not be said of the Franciscans. What the military had gained with one hand, the Franciscans did their best to give away with another.

A case in point was the imprisoned chief held in San Francisco. The Franciscans, fretting about his immortal soul, would not leave well enough alone. And the chief, like any good warrior, sought to exploit the division he perceived to exist among the Spaniards. He began to profess love for what he had earlier been risking his life to destroy. The Franciscans sensed an imminent conversion where the military saw only a tactical ploy. The Franciscan missionary prevailed upon the San Francisco commander for more humane treatment of the prisoner, now that he was a potential brother in Christ. The commandante, against his better judgment, allowed the chief more freedom. And the chief used this freedom not to go to chapel, but to steal a horse. He eventually made his way back to Marin, and the pacification of the peninsula had to begin all over again.

Such at least was Vallejo's account of the origin of the troubles at Mission San Rafael which culminated in the attack of 1824. It was the gullible Franciscans' own fault. With the attack of 1824, according to Vallejo, the military finally gained a free hand to deal with the hostiles. The escaped chief was trapped near the northern sea coast of the peninsula. A lieutenant, named Pompiono, escaped with part of the band; but eventually he too was captured in one of the remote, dry valleys of northern Marin.

The chief was again taken to San Francisco, and incarcerated. Once again, he professed love of things European. He converted to Christianity. And when everyone was convinced that the conversion was sincere, he was allowed to return to the Marin Peninsula where he lived out the remainder of his days as an exemplary mission native.

The fate of his lieutenant Pompiono might have influenced the sincerity of his second repentance. Pompiono was taken to Monterey, formally tried, condemned, and shot. On the board that condemned him was Mariano Vallejo.

When Vallejo himself moved to the north bay, his plan was to use his arms not to suppress the native tribes in the region, but to assist them in suppressing the tribes further north which had been their traditional enemies. By his own account, the north bay chiefs enthusiastically accepted his approach.

This, of course, meant at times allowing his allies to have their own way with the defeated peoples, however much this might outrage more delicate European sensibilities. One European rancher who had early established himself near Vallejo told a story of going on one such raid against a northern village with Vallejo and Stone Hands, Vallejo's most important native ally. After the battle was won, Stone Hands saw a pregnant woman running away with a baby on her back. He rode after her with his horse. As he got close, he lanced the baby at her back; and as he rode past, he ripped open her stomach with his sword. The European rancher instinctively raised his rifle to shoot the chief. The barrel was grabbed by Vallejo who smiled and said, "He is the best friend I have." There was nothing to do; Vallejo was, the rancher explained, a law unto himself—nothing to do, that is, except sell his ranch and move south.

Many Europeans, who perhaps had not seen Vallejo and Solano in action, were not so reluctant to be beholden to him for their well being. Vallejo was not only the chief military commander of the north bay; he also had the effective power to dispose of its mission wealth as he saw fit, once the order for secularization was formally given.

When the secularization order for San Rafael came, Vallejo

apparently stripped the mission of everything he wanted. Substantial portions of the mission herds, even the best of the vineyard, were taken to Vallejo's ranch in Sonoma. Mariano Vallejo was able to do to Mission San Rafael, and later to Mission San Francisco Solano, what the Estudillos of California had only dreamt of doing. Compared to their Quixotes, he was a Cortes.

The friars were now, at last, helpless. When Moreno interferred with Vallejo's diplomacy, Vallejo could simply have him removed. And when Vallejo wished to do with Mission San Francisco Solano as he wanted, Friar Quijas could only move to the ruins of Mission San Rafael. There he would at least be physically separated from the malefactor Vallejo, but there he would still be dependent for his very sustenance upon a mission administrator who was in effect an appointee of Vallejo.

The Franciscans had now been finally defeated, and the conquest of California, its complete control by the race of reason would now be achieved. A new social order would be established, a republican order in which Vallejo and those like him would be first citizens. Vallejo *was* the first citizen of the north bay. To him and those under him, this region owed its security—and now the missions had rewarded him properly for his large and continuing service. At last the Church had been forced to render to Caesar what was his by right.

Vallejo also saw clearly what was required to effect this new, stable social order. The mission lands had to be divided up among citizens loyal to the new order of things. In this division of mission lands north of the bay, Vallejo wished only that the grantees be loyal to the California government in Monterey, and also be indebted to him for having interceded with that government for them.

The mission lands claimed by Juan Amoros and his successors for San Rafael and its neophytes comprised virtually all the Marin Peninsula. From this claim only the southernmost tip of the peninsula and the wilds of Point Reyes were omitted. Now all the peninsula was to be divided up into large ranches. Rather than having one huge mission stifling development by its commitment to a divine order of things, there would be a series of ranches averaging about ten thousand acres each. What the mission did but once, the ranches could do ten or twenty times over. The church could attend to the development of things spiritual while the rancher attended to the development of things material.

But this transition would take time. In 1835 less than one dozen people of reason lived on the Marin Peninsula. At least ten times that number would be needed to control an area as large as Marin. It would take time to select the right men for the land grants, time for them to get settled, to establish their ranches, to build up their herds. It would take at least a decade, perhaps even two.

The Christian natives would need particular attention during this transition. The new system would depend as much upon their labor as had the old mission system. They would simply be supervised by ranchers now rather than by friars. They would be better off. They would have more freedom in their personal conduct than they had before, and would find their position as ranch hands more comfortable than that as mission neophytes. Twenty ranches would civilize the Marin native more effectively than had one mission. Eventually the gentiles as well would be absorbed by the ranches.

The Christian natives needed particular assistance through this transition because there was the awkward matter of their rights. The neophytes knew, or at least their leaders knew, that secularization was being undertaken in their name. The Mexican authorities had attempted to divide the neophytes from their missionaries by telling them that secularization would give them wealth. And the desperate friars had countered by harranging them that outside of the protection of the Church they would be at the mercy of European predators, what little mission wealth they did receive would soon be taken away.

The situation could be awkward, but time was on Vallejo's side. These natives were not very intelligent, not true people of reason. All Vallejo had to do was to buy time with promises. The longer he could temporize, the more European ranches in Marin and Sonoma, the more dispersed the native population at these ranches, the weaker the position of the native chiefs should they be tempted to follow the path of Pompiono.

In 1835 the neophytes of San Rafael were given their choice of mission lands by Vallejo, as legally required in the order of secularization. They chose well, a large inland valley called Nicasio in the north of the peninsula. On March 13, 1835, the governor of California ordered Vallejo to "notify the said christianized Indians that the government in consequence of the preference they are entitled to and of their right to have lands for colonization does grant to them in full ownership the said land above mentioned called Nicasio."

Vallejo conveyed to them title to the land and also a small portion of the mission wealth—all of which was theirs by right.

The Governor had also ordered Vallejo to insure that "none disturb" the Nicasio Indians, perhaps not realizing that the person of reason most likely to disturb the Nicasio Indians for his own designs was Mariano Vallejo himself. Two years after the grant, Vallejo on his own authority declared that the natives were "not making good use of the property that had been distributed." So he collected it, and assured the natives that it would be returned to them "when circumstances should be more favorable."

When by August, 1839, the conditions were still not favorable in Vallejo's judgment, three Indian leaders appealed directly to the governor. However, the governor who had granted them the land was now dead; and the man who now occupied that position happened also to be Mariano Vallejo's nephew. "We pray your excellency to take into consideration that we are poor and have large families so that you may be pleased to help and protect us." The governor responded that he was pleased, pleased to inform them that they could certainly rely upon the protection of Mariano Vallejo.

This response seems to have been enough to have brought the ex-neophytes to armed rebellion. But Vallejo knew the use of tactical retreat. Now he gave the chiefs a new legal title to some land, althought it was only a small portion of Nicasio (and subsequently would not stand a court test). He also returned three cattle and one horse to each native. He had bought himself more time.

When in 1841 an inspector from the Monterey government unexpectedly arrived in Marin to see how secularization was progressing there, he found the situation at San Rafael worse even than elsewhere. His interviews with the ex-neophytes served to cause excitement where Vallejo only wished calm. Before the inspector could complete his crossing of San Francisco Bay out of Vallejo's realm, he was intercepted by Vallejo's men, and forcibly returned so that Mariano might have the opportunity to reason with him.

The inspector while honest was also prudent. He did make some general suggestions about San Rafael and other missions; he also shortly after resigned his position as inspector. And the Monterey government, perhaps recognizing its impotence against local barons like Vallejo, failed to appoint a replacement.

By 1843 virtually the whole Marin Peninsula had been allocated to people of reason, virtually all except Nicasio. In November,

1843, two people of reason sought to correct this oversight; apparently without Vallejo's knowledge they appealed to the governor for title to Nicasio. (One of these men already owned a tract of land in Marin, a redwood forest assigned to him earlier by the governor, apparently in repayment for a personal debt.)

Now Vallejo had to act quickly, lest prime Marin ranch land fall into the hands of men not beholden to him for it. Apparently he convinced the chiefs of Nicasio that only his good will could preserve their land for them. In December Vallejo himself wrote a petition on their behalf to the new governor (no longer his nephew). He petitioned that these industrious, loyal natives be granted title to Nicasio, and that "I may have the pleasure of delivering it to them."

When almost a year passed with no word, Vallejo decided to force the Monterey governor's hand. (And perhaps also to use his silence to get more out of all this than he originally intended.) On October 14, 1844, the Nicasio chiefs were formally presented by Mariano Vallejo with title to their lands—something, of course, he had no legal power to do. On October 15, 1844, these chiefs formally gave the title to their eighty thousand acres to the same nephew who as governor had assured them they could rely on Mariano. In repayment for this title, Mariano, not his nephew, agreed to pay them one thousand dollars. The chiefs then signed a receipt for the money which apparently they had never received. The nephew then sent in his claim to Nicasio to Monterey for its ratification.

It could be argued that Vallejo had simply outwitted the chiefs once again. Stories are told that they were drunk when they signed the agreement and receipt or that they could not read what they signed. Yet, even if they were fully aware of what they were doing, what were their alternatives? Their own attempt to get title to their land had apparently failed, even with Vallejo's help. They seemed confronted with a choice between having the land owned by total strangers or having it effectively controlled by Vallejo. They knew Vallejo; he had always professed their interest; and what wealth they possessed had come from his hands. He thought he could still gain title to the land if they would sign it over to his nephew, the ex-governor. He said the money would make the agreement look better to European eyes. They did not care about money; they only wished that some of their land and cattle might remain theirs. And Vallejo and his relative would be more likely to have to honor that paper for a portion of their land he had given them years before.

In short, perhaps the chiefs did act intelligently. It was a desperate situation from which the most they could hope to emerge with was the portion of their land on which they lived. They found themselves exposed on the unfamiliar terrain of politics and law, European politics and law. And they were confronted with grizzlies that threatened to devour them and their families. Coyote man would not fight in such a hopeless situation, if he could help it; he would rather seek another grizzly with which to ally, and would hope that after the crisis had passed this grizzly would not turn on him. It could have been a shrewd calculation.

However, when Vallejo's nephew filed his legal claim for title to Nicasio, the secretary of state informed the governor that the natives "could not transfer to another person a right they did not possess." The secretary had detected that the whole exchange had been engineered by Mariano Vallejo, in the secretary's word, "fraudulently." But he only observed that fact by the way. More than six months before the native chiefs had been given their title by Vallejo, the California government had assigned the land to the earlier petitioners. These men, therefore, are "the owners and sole proprietors of the land Nicasio."

For one of the first times, Vallejo had been clearly outmaneuvered. His nephew still tried to occupy the land with his herds; the new owners simply ignored him, since they had not intended to use the land anyway. The chiefs and their people were also permitted to stay, for the time being. But they were now legally a landless people, trespassing on the peninsula of their fathers.

Among the few surviving myths of the Marin natives, there is only one that attempts to account for their decline. It explained "why nearly all died soon after the whiteman came."

When Coyote man decided to make people, he made them magically from wood. Wherever he wanted a village of people, Coyote man would put some sticks, and these sticks somehow would soon be transformed into people. But the sticks were not all the same. Some bunches of sticks were from strong trees like the oak; others were from brush, and were soft and hollow. The whitemen were lucky; they sprang from hard wood, and hence were "strong and well and warm-blooded and could stand cold weather." But for some reason Coyote man chose to have the Indians spring from brush; so it is that "we are hollow inside and cannot stand the cold." That is the reason "our people are tender and weak and cannot stand the cold, and why nearly all died soon after the whiteman came."

In this myth they told a biological truth about themselves and the other California natives. They had no immunities to European diseases, and were in that respect biologically weak and hollow. But the myth, if unintentionally, also told a truth about Europeans like Vallejo, a truth broader than the biological. A Mariano Vallejo, priding himself on his superior intelligence and prowess, was hard at his core.

If the chiefs did make a decisive mistake in their handling of their people's affairs after secularization, they made it long before the land deal of 1843. They had to play coyote long before they did. They had to play him long before the situation had become desperate, when there was still time to be the trickster. None of the chiefs who led their people to Nicasio understood this. But one Marin chief did. He was the true Coyote man of the peninsula. His name was Camilo Ynitia.

All nineteenth century European memoirs that mention Ynitia praise him. He had accepted European ways early. He dressed like a person of reason. Everyone noted his cleanliness. All these sources also note that Camilo inherited his openness to civilization from his father.

According to a story often repeated, the first European exploration party up the small river that forms the natural northern boundary of the Marin Peninsula met an extraordinarily friendly tribe at a village called by the natives Olompali. The chief of the village was Camilo's father. The chief made the Europeans so welcome that they felt they should do something for him in return. So they showed him how to make adobe, and built him a small adobe house to replace his hut. In 1840 Camilo Ynitia still lived in the house, portions of which had been built by the Spaniards for his father.

The story of Camilo Ynitia's father is repeated in most nineteenth and early twentieth century accounts of Marin history. And well it might be. It is a far happier story than Pompiono's unrelenting opposition to the Europeans, or even of his chief's eventual conversion. It is the story of a native family who met the Europeans from the first in open friendship. It is a story of Europeans who, unlike those involved with Nicasio, reciprocated in friendship, and helped the grateful natives as any good Christian should. It is a story of European-native contact as any European would like to think it actually had been, at least once. It is also a story that is demonstrably a fabrication.

From the diaries of that expedition it is clear that the Spaniards were not there long enough to build any adobe house for any native chief, even if they had made contact with one. Moreover, they record no contact with any natives, a fact the chaplain would not have forgotten, particularly if they seemed likely subjects for conversion. The story of Camilo Ynitia's father is a fabrication, and it is not difficult to guess who fabricated it.

It must have been a favorite story of the European ranchers as they took over more and more of the peninsula. And over the years, as he adopted more and more of the ways of the Europeans, Camilo Ynitia must have become very adept at the telling of it, just as the elders of his father's village had become in times past very adept at telling stories of Coyote man outwitting the grizzly.

Camilo Ynitia not only knew what stories to tell the Europeans; he also knew to which Europeans to tell them. Ynitia's closest European friend was Mariano Vallejo. And, after Stone Hands, Ynitia was Vallejo's closest native friend. That Vallejo might prefer Stone Hands to Ynitia is understandable, since there is no record of Ynitia accompanying Vallejo and Solano on military expeditions. Remarkably, Ynitia managed to get Vallejo's good graces without risking his life for them.

In 1843, the same year the Nicasio chiefs petitioned for their land, Camilo Ynitia himself applied. He knew better than to try for anything like the eighty thousand acres they naively hoped to get. He asked for little more than eight thousand, most of it worthless land, but with one good valley and a little frontage on the bay. It was enough for Ynitia and his immediate family to live comfortably on; and it had on it the adobe walls the Europeans had made for his father decades before. Surely it could not be given to anyone else?

Ynitia was granted his request for Olompali and the land surrounding it. Coyote man had gained one small victory. At Olompali Ynitia would run cattle, a herd of more than five hundred head. He would sell his excess products, occasionally even to the Russians. Everyone who had done business with him said he was a shrewd bargainer. Although Camilo Ynitia never learned to sign his name, he apparently did find time to learn to keep accounts.

Camilo Ynitia lived to see the Yankee take-over. In fact, he was at one point taken captive by a Yankee raiding party. The Yankees, at least as Ynitia told the story shortly after, could not decide whether or not to incarcerate him; finally he convinced them that his skin was more important than his sombrero: he was no Mexican. (Ynitia, shortly before, had been serving breakfast to Mexican troops.)

After the Yankee take-over, Ynitia saw all the Mexican land titles enmeshed in American legal technicalities that not even Vallejo fully understood. His own land title in fact became involved in an appeal. So it was that Coyote man played a last trick before he died.

Ynitia sold his disputed rights to Olompali for five thousand dollars, which he immediately converted into gold. He also sold much of his livestock, and once again converted the money into gold. And then, according to the story, he buried the gold.

The Europeans who subsequently told of Camilo's life claimed that at this point he had finally out-foxed himself. A brother, jealous of Camilo's riches, shot him dead in a corral. Camilo had neglected to tell his wife and two daughters the exact location of the buried gold. Thus, what had been guilefully accumulated and preserved throughout his life was, by too much guile, lost to his family at his death.

It was a wonderful story, that of Camilo's death. It must have been popular at a time when so many of the original settlers of Marin were losing their wealth to Yankee squatters and lawyers. Even Camilo Ynitia, always one step ahead, had finally outwitted himself. Not even old Coyote man could preserve himself from this catastrophe.

In fact, the story is so good that one would be forgiven if he thought he saw the hand of a master storyteller at work. The one Marin native who managed to run free was finally killed in jealousy by one of his own in a corral. The corral was such a nice, even delicate touch. The jealousy was too. Of course, if Ynitia had managed to preserve his wealth through the Yankee take-over, the Indians who had been dispossessed for so long would not be those who most resented his success. Those most resentful would be the European settlers who were themselves losing everything. These settlers might well have been quite resentful if Ynitia, who had his wealth only at their caprice, should emerge prosperous from it all. They could make life difficult for Ynitia's family, particularly if he was no longer there to mollify them.

But Ynitia could survive his own death, as a guardian spirit, through his stories. One would like to think of Camilo Ynitia on his death bed recounting a last tale for his family to share with the outside world after his passing—perhaps even rehearsing them in the telling of it, scolding them if they left out the nice touches like the corral, and certainly smiling when they got it right, pleased with himself.

What is known is that Camilo Ynitia died in 1856, in his bed, surrounded by his family, and almost certainly from natural causes. His financial affairs were, as usual, in order. Less than a year before, he had drawn up a will with a local justice of the peace, a Harvard man who would soon marry one of Camilo's daughters. Not long after his death his family moved away from the Marin Peninsula. They bought a ranch farther to the north. They returned to Marin only to buy a large herd to stock this ranch. It was said they paid for it in gold. But people knew better than to believe so unlikely a tale.

The triumph of Camilo Ynitia was a singular triumph, in which others of his people could only participate vicariously, if at all. In the Mexican order there was not room for many Ynitias. His shrewdness consisted in recognizing that there was room for one.

Among the ranchers themselves, tales began to be handed down about the natives of old, who were so different from the decaying race they saw about them. To the name Pompiono, for instance, became attached tales of proverbial bravery and savagery connected with the native resistance to Europeans. Once Pompiono was caught and placed in leg irons. Somehow he managed to get a knife. When his captors came in next morning, all they found was the leg iron, a portion of Pompiono's heel, and a trail of blood. This particular story was not only told of Pompiono, but also of a nameless brave in his band. (And, for that matter, it also appears in Herodotus.)

Once Pompiono and a supporter (perhaps the same one who had earlier cut off his heel) were on horseback being pursued by the military. The brave was wounded and fell from his horse. He had once been a neophyte and had learned enough of his catechism to know what happened to someone who died in mortal sin. He began calling for a priest. Pompiono, hearing his friend, turned his horse, rode back at considerable risk, and lanced him to death.

Such viciousness eventually cost Pompiono his life, at least according to one account. After his final capture, he was in no danger of being executed. Although much had been attributed to him, no capital crime could be proven. Pompiono, in his irrational hatred of all things European, could never believe this, but European law would have preserved his life. However, on the way to Monterey, he murdered one of his guards, not because he had any chance to escape, but just out of viciousness. This was the crime for which he was executed.

Pompiono's captured chief became in story the good native leader who after initial opposition recognizes the superiority of European ways. Fittingly, the greatest warrior chief of Marin was himself adept on water. He was almost captured once during his attacks on the mission in the early 1820s, but took to the water and escaped by maneuvering ably about the small bay islands off the Marin coast. According to other stories, these islands provided the chief with his hide-out. At any rate, after the chief became a good native, he was supposed to have endeavored to serve the Europeans with his talents. He became a pilot on the bay for the Europeans. So adept was he on the treacherous bay waters that in gratitude the Europeans came to call him "el marinero," the mariner.

Eventually this name was shortened. He was such a good native, so brave in his earlier resistance, so prudent in his eventual yielding, so exemplary in his present service. He was the Marin native as Europeans wished to imagine him. Pompiono would share his name only with the remote canyon where he was supposed to have been finally captured; but all the peninsula would share its name with the mariner chief. He, in his servitude, was to be known as Chief Marin. And some would say that the peninsula did not share its name with him, but he shared his with it.

Needless to say, as many stories attached themselves to the name Chief Marin as did to Pompiono. In fact, some of the same stories did. For instance, Pompiono and his brave, it seems, were not the only Indians limping about the peninsula. Nonetheless, there was one notable story told about Chief Marin in his later years, allegedly by an eyewitness, who told it to show the persistence of native superstition.

Natives were needed to assist a surveyor mapping the area around Mount Tamalpais, so long hostile, now suitable for European settlement. Chief Marin was an obvious choice, both because he was so eager to help his new masters and also because he knew the place well from earlier, different times. At one point the surveyor, Marin and two other natives reached a ridge in view of the highest peak of Mount Tamalpais. Marin insisted they should go no further. When the surveyor asked why (probably expecting to hear of rattlesnakes or grizzly bears), Marin explained that the high ground was sacred, powerful spirits still inhabited it, any man who trespassed would died. The other natives agreed.

The surveyor had heard enough. He was going to disabuse them of this superstition. Although they would not accompany him, he was going to break this taboo himself. He was going to climb to the peak so they could be done with this nonsense and get on with their work. The Indians promised to wait for him to return, although privately they were likely trying to think how they would explain his loss to the friar, who did not understand such things.

When the surveyor returned, they would not believe that he had actually reached the top. But then he pointed out a wooden cross he had fashioned and placed there. Now Chief Marin was in a quandary. He did not want to climb Mount Tamalpais. Nonetheless, he had his reputation, at least among the mission natives, of being the bravest of the brave. He could not allow a European to excel him. So off he went up the mountain himself to meet his death. (That evil spirits did not trouble with Europeans did not make them any less virulent for him.)

Much later he too returned, bare chested. First his fellow braves thought him the ghost of his former self. Then they refused to believe that he had actually made it to the summit. The spirits must have chased him away, and stolen the red shirt the friar had given him. They had done no such thing, Marin insisted. He had left it as a sign of his triumph. When they looked to the summit, they saw that what he said was true. The red shirt the friar had given him was hung on the cross.

V
Murphy's Day

Rafael Garcia had made Joseph Revere a generous offer. The American, on leave from the naval vessel where he was a lieutenant, had been travelling through the western Marin Peninsula to see the sights when the Mexican rancher told him of the elk herds nearer the coast. For weeks the elk had been gorging themselves on wild oats; now they were too fat to outmaneuver a California horseman. Garcia and a few friends were going out after them, and Revere was welcome to come along if he wished.

As Revere rode off with the hospitable Californians in search of elk, he discovered to his surprise that they seemed even less adequately equipped than he was. One of the Californians had a knife tied by rawhide to a long pole—"la luna," they called it, after the crescent shape of the blade. The rest of the party was, as far as Revere could see, entirely unarmed. When he asked his host about this, the Californian simply pointed to his riata, the rawhide rope slung over his saddle horn. "This is the rancher's rifle," Garcia said, a remark that Revere found perplexing: elk was big game.

The hunters soon came upon an elk herd which in Revere's awed estimate numbered more than four hundred animals. But the Californians did not seem to be the slightest bit impressed, nor did they make an effort to conceal their presence. The small party fanned out, and rode slowly toward the herd, giving the elk ample time to retreat.

Eventually the elk could retreat no more, for the land had ended in cliffs falling down into the sea. The hunters, by their slow, seemingly menaceless approach, had trapped a portion of the herd between themselves and the empty space above the sea. Finally, too late, the remaining elk sensed the danger. When these tried to move back toward the open range, two horsemen charged, one the Californian with the luna. Everything after that happened quickly.

"Our friend with the luna had hamstrung several of the poor creatures, and his companion had entangled with his riata a noble buck, which was plunging and tearing violently, the riata being at its greatest tension, and the little horse, to whose saddle it was made fast, standing stiff and stark, with eye-balls staring, and every nerve braced to meet the pulls and tugs of the elk; while the Californian sat coolly in his saddle, and addressing the elk by the familiar title of 'cunado', (brother-in-law), pleasantly assured him that he 'only wanted a little of his lard wherewithal to cook tortillas!'—a joke which the struggling victim was in no humor to relish."

The other men now joined in the hunt, and Revere soon saw the effectiveness of the rancher's rifle, even against big game. Two skillful horsemen using riatas alone could kill an elk with little apparent difficulty; one to trip him up, the other to administer the *coup de grace*. And, Revere learned, there are "rare instances where a single expert hand trips up the animal with his riata and then finishes him" with the same riata.

Naturally, the luna was more efficient: first the animal would be hamstrung, then its neck veins opened. But in a land like California, where game was so plentiful, so easy to take, efficiency could be sacrificed to increase the sport, and thereby to enhance the dignity of predator and prey alike. Always to use a scythe to harvest elk was too easy, too much like farming. The best bull elk should be allowed to perform his dance of death, with his proud muscles intact, at the end of a hide rope pulled taut by a fellow grazer. Let him die in the sun strangled by his own strength.

When the excitement was over, and the last of the hamstrung elk dispatched, the hunting party carried or dragged six of their nine elk back toward Garcia's ranch. (A doe and her fawn, and also a hamstrung bull that had fallen into the surf below, were left behind for the scavenging birds, which as Revere and the Californians rode off were already hovering over the dying bull.) Garcia's ranch, like the hunt, had its surprises for the Yankee who had not been in California long. The cattle near the ranch seemed as wild as the deer and antelope with which they freely mingled in their grazing. The ranch itself was little more than a broken down corral. And, once the hunters were within sight of it, Indians descended upon them from all sides—they must have sensed the fresh blood, Revere thought, "like vultures, by instinct."

Revere soon learned that the Indians were coming not merely to scavenge. They dragged the elk carcasses the remaining distance to the "ranch." They skinned and butchered them. The next day Revere would watch the Indians prepare the hide and render the fat so that it could be stored as tallow. But now was the time for a celebration of the hunt. And so the Indians prepared a barbecue of the choice parts of the elk. Then Indian laborers and European hunters sat down together for a feast of fresh meat.

"The savory saddle, the juicy and tender haunch, the delicious rib were all discussed in turn, and such as liked it feasted on the lucious liver—a most delicate morsel—and also on the kidney and brains." Revere imitated his companions and "gorged myself." Then the hunters passed brandy among themselves, and their day was over. "We all wrapped ourselves in serapes and blankets; stretched out upon the ground with our feet to the fire—while the silvery moon stole over the inland mountains and bathed us in serenest light—we fell asleep."

Or rather the ranchers' day was over. The Indians continued to celebrate; and Revere, despite his weariness, his full stomach, the brandy, was a Yankee unaccustomed to sharing the moon with such savages. And so while the Californian hunters slept oblivious, Revere listened in the night to what sounded to his more sensitive ears to be "hideous orgies," "infernal clamor."

"The fat of the land"—this was the phrase one of the old-timers used to recreate the ranch life in Marin for those who had never seen it first hand, those for whom stories of elk herds on the peninsula would seem to be tall tales. Life was lived on a different scale in the old days, Charlie Lauff insisted. There was more than enough for everyone in those days, and so everyone was carefree. "We lived off the fat of the land," he said, "and never worried tomorrow."

The material basis for the life that seemed to Lauff and others simple bliss was the California range. On the Marin Peninsula, as throughout California, this range had not been fully used by the native grazing herds of elk, deer, and antelope. A Yankee like Revere might be impressed by the size of a Marin elk herd, but such herds were miniscule compared to the buffalo herds supported by the comparable range lands of the Great Plains.

This was one reason the herds of mission livestock had increased so rapidly. Initially at least, they did not have to compete with native herds for forage; there was more than enough for both. Jedediah Smith, the very first overland traveler to California who passed from the Great Plains to the Pacific coast in 1826, was struck by the similarity between a mission herd and the buffalo herds he had recently left. Yet such a comparison, however apt in one respect, was misleading in another. The mission system was incapable, and indeed unwilling, to exploit fully the ranching potential of the California range.

For instance, although Mission San Rafael claimed almost the whole of the Marin Peninsula as its own land, the single missionary with the few soldiers assigned to him could not supervise the development of an extensive ranching operation. The mission herds, in practice, would be restricted to the best grazing land easily accessible to the mission. However large the mission herd might appear when viewed in isolation, it left most of the Marin range untouched.

And the missionaries themselves did not, on the whole, regret this. They were attempting to transform hunters and gatherers into Christians who led a regulated life. The daily rhythm of agriculture assisted more in this transformation than did the sporadic labor of ranching, which had too much in common with the neophytes' older way of life. The neophytes did have their daily meat, but this meat was found in small pieces in a porridge of grain and vegetables.

The missions, in short, displayed the ranching potential of the California range without fully exploiting it. And this was a strong argument among progressives in California like Vallejo for ending the missions' land monopoly. Once the missions were secularized in 1834, prospective ranchers fanned out to establish cattle herds on every suitable portion of the land. The immediate results were, even to those who had seen the growth of mission herds, stunning.

On Angel Island, for example, the same island Ayala had used as a base in 1775, one rancher in 1839 placed a herd of approximately fifty head. Even so small a herd must have seemed to some a little optimistic. The island was less than seven hundred and fifty acres, much of that mountainous and shrub-covered, much of the rest heavily forested. Moreover, because of a lack of predators, there was already a sizable deer population. Nonetheless, within seven years that same herd, tended by only a single cowboy, was reported to have grown from fifty to five hundred head. Even if the report was

somewhat exaggerated, the enlarged herd was truly the fat of
the land.

This was why a rancher apparently did not have to worry tomorrow. The land seemed quite willing to produce more fat than he
could use. The land was, in the rancher's eyes, like a perfect brother-
in-law, industrious, wealthy, and generous. The rancher had only to
bless his good fortune at having married into such a family.

Only twice a year would extended labor be required. Once a
year there would be a round-up to collect strays and brand calves.
Once a year there would be a major slaughter of cattle to provide
dried meat, hides, and tallow, a slaughter which differed little from
an elk hunt.

And from most of this labor the rancher and his family were
spared. All sources that comment on this subject (and most ignore it
entirely) agree with the Marin rancher who remembered that the
"Indians did nearly all of the work of the country." Another witness
wrote, "Throughout California the Indians are the principal laborers;
without them the business of the country could hardly be carried on."
Another said, "Among the Mexicans there is no working class (the
Indians being practically serfs, and doing all the hard work)."

In particular, the Indians practiced the arts taught them by the
friars. They were the ones who raised the vegetables and tended
the orchards. They made the adobe and kept it in repair. It was they
who skinned the carcass, and butchered it and melted the fat and
dried the meat and worked the rawhide. The rancher or his wife
would usually supervise, but the Indians would do the labor.

Thus the California rancher did not have to worry tomorrow.
The land produced more fat than he could possibly use, and it also
provided hands to prepare the fat for his use. The Indians were but
an extension of his family, and the land an extension of them. And
the rancher's position as pater familias was unchallenged. Or so it
seemed in the idyllic recollections of ranch life by Lauff and others.

Yet there was one disturbing element. Nature, even in these
accounts, gave the otherwise blest rancher an occasional glimpse of
its lunar gloom. This was provided by the grizzly bear.

The natives had scrupulously yielded most of the peninsula to
the grizzly. All of their villages were on open land near water. They
penetrated its normal haunts with reluctance; when it penetrated
their normal ground—to gorge itself on ripe acorns, for instance—
they simply waited their turn.

This situation had been only slightly changed by the missionaries; the Franciscans established their mission on the bay near large villages of likely converts. The occasional grizzly that would harrass mission livestock would be shot; but the missionaries were, in practice, content to allow the remote areas of the peninsula to remain an infernal realm of gentiles and grizzlies.

The ranchers, in contrast, could not be satisfied with a mere human beachhead. They wanted their herds to be free to roam the whole peninsula in search of good grazing. Their annual roundups would have to sweep practically the whole peninsula except the highest ground and the deepest forest. The new and old grazers might be able to mingle together in peace; such could not happen between the new and old carnivores. Theirs was to be, at least from the human side, a state of perpetual war.

The war had in fact begun long before the first ranch was established, at a time the mission itself was only a plan. The *Albatross*, which records in its log the beginning of the extermination of the Marin fur seals, also contains the first recorded encounter between a grizzly bear and a European on the Marin Peninsula. Two crewmen, put ashore to replenish the ship's meat supply, shot a grizzly at close range. Before the bear died, it had severely mauled one of the men. The log entry notes that crewman Jerry Bancroft was going to survive his wounds; it adds, "The bear proved good eating."

By the late 1830s such attacks were no longer isolated incidents. As one visitor to the Marin Peninsula in the 1840s put it, "There is scarcely a resident in the mountains of upper California who had not at one time or another been attacked by these formidable beasts." Another traveler in this period arrived at San Rafael shortly after a particularly severe bear mauling had occurred.

"Mr. Daniel Sill was nearly killed by a bear a few days since. He, being hunting and seeing a number of bear about, got off his horse to shoot one, and, while crawling up to get within range of one, another, which he had not seen, rushed out from the bushes alongside him and caught him by his thigh. And tearing away the flesh caught him by the arm which he lacerated most horribly and undoubtedly would have supped off his body had not Sill by a fortunate kick in a private part caused Mr. Bruin to release his grip for a moment; when Sill, seizing his rifle, shot him through the jaws."

Encounters with grizzlies were remembered, and gradually transformed into stories more memorable still. Timothy Murphy, for instance, had an unforgettable encounter with a grizzly bear. Murphy was, in Charlie Lauff's judgment, king of the peninsula. He had, with the approval of Vallejo, taken over administration of the mission property after John Reed; eventually the best mission grazing land found its way into Murphy's hands. Throughout the ranch period, Murphy occupied San Rafael, the traditional center of European life on the peninsula. As such, he was first among equals, and enjoyed playing, if not the king, at least the baron of the region.

Geography was not the only reason for Murphy's prominence. Murphy himself was a formidable presence, well over six feet tall, weighing in excess of three hundred pounds. He was the strongest man on the peninsula, and reputed to be the best shot with a rifle. In short, he was a likely choice to be the human champion in single combat with a grizzly.

The confrontation, as it actually occurred, does not seem to have been enobling for either side. One traveler was told of it not long after it occurred. According to this version, Murphy had been torn from his saddle by the bear. Murphy knew enough not to fight. He simply "feigned death until his friends, who were in sight, came up and drove balls into the beast." The claws of the grizzly had left deep wounds in Murphy's back; years later the scars would still be visible. But it was the jaws that had caused the lasting fright; throughout most of the time Murphy had been on the ground the grizzly's jaws had been within two inches of his face. He had felt the grizzly's breath on his cheeks.

Out of this incident there evolved a tall tale which celebrates the triumph of a rancher over a bear, of human spunk over mindless destructiveness. To transform the original encounter into a triumph for humanity, many of the details had to be reshaped, some drastically.

Timothy Murphy, in the polished tale, is not unceremoniously dragged from his horse. Rather his horse betrays him; the horse, frightened by the unexpected appearance of a bear, throws Murphy. Nonetheless, Murphy still manages to remain master of the situation. When the bear attacks, Murphy, far from playing dead, grabs the bear in a hug, and knees it again and again in what the tale specifies as the bear's stomach. The bear and Murphy roll over and over in Murphy's grasp until finally the bear breaks free. It realizes that the day is Murphy's, and runs off.

We lived off the fat of the land, old Charlie Lauff had said, we lived off the fat of the land without worrying tomorrow. Anyone who understands the connection between tall bear tales, ample Indian servants, and bountifully increasing cattle herds understands much of what he meant by this—and understands too how a hunter could address his prey as *cunado.*

As nature was generous to the ranchers with their ever increasing herds, so also were the ranchers generous with the truth in their ever enlarging bear stories. And so too were they generous to those good guests who would listen to the stories. The treatment of guests at California ranches was proverbial in its openhandedness.

A passing guest would be given food, lodging, a horse, supplies, or whatever else he needed that was at hand. In the guest rooms of the larger ranches there would be a small dish of money from which he could take whatever he thought he would need. This need was more psychological than anything else. The saying was that someone could travel the whole length of California on nothing beyond good manners. And even manners might not be necessary.

"Their hospitality knows no bounds. Were the Devil himself to call for a night's lodging, the Californian would hardly find it in his heart to bolt the door. He would think they could manage against his horns, hoofs, and tail in some way." Or so said one guest who had partaken of the food and the spirit of the place.

The Mexican government was equally generous with land grants to its citizens residing in California. Almost any citizen willing to occupy and improve previously unoccupied California land could have thousands of acres granted to him if he only petitioned. To show his willingness to live and develop his desired land, a prospective rancher, about the time he made his petition, would usually build a temporary house on it. This house would almost always be what the Californians called a palizida: walls of logs plastered with mud, a roof of tules. When the final grant was received, the rancher would then build an adobe house (and usually give the palizida to his foreman). The spread of ranches throughout the Marin Peninsula in a given period can, therefore, be roughly measured by the number of new palizidas and adobes built.

In 1834, the year of secularization, there was not a single adobe building on the Marin Peninsula except for the seventeen that constituted the mission compound; the only palizida on the rest of the peninsula was that of John Reed. In the next five years, by 1839, seven new palizidas had been slapped together; the only new adobe was that into which John Reed had moved his family. By ten years after secularization, much of the peninsula had been granted by the government; as a result, there were, between 1839 and 1844, a dozen new adobes erected, while the number of new palizidas declined slightly to five. By 1846, the year of Revere's elk hunt, the secular adobes of the Marin Peninsula finally outnumbered those now collapsing into ruins at the old mission.

Generous as the land policy of the Mexican government was, the ranchers were able to infuse even its few legalisms with their own generous spirit. If ranchers could let their herds run wild, they had no reason to trouble over these formalities, however imposing they might look from Mexico City.

The case of Rafael Garcia, who led Revere's elk hunt, is sufficient to show the distance between theory and practice in the allocation of California ranch land. Initially, Garcia was scrupulous in his pursuit of title. He occupied the land at the southern end of Point Reyes, near the coyote's chest. He built a palizida, and ran his herds. Once he had established himself, he petitioned the government for a formal grant of the land, including in his petition all that the government wanted. He could also appeal to his own military record, which included service at Mission San Rafael. (He also commanded the Spanish troops in the battle recorded by Vallejo in which the Indian village and its inhabitants were destroyed by fire.) The case was exemplary, and a grant of more than 8,000 acres was soon given.

The complications began when Garcia invited his sister and her husband to join his family at his new ranch. He soon decided that the ranch was not big enough for both families. So Garcia gave the ranch to his brother-in-law, moved his own herds a little farther north on the peninsula, built a house there, and petitioned for land a second time.

All this was, one can imagine, done in the openhanded, generous spirit of the growing ranch society. Most all of it also happened to be of questionable legality. Garcia had no clear right to transfer his land grant to his brother-in-law; nonetheless, the government acquiesced to the transfer. But that was not the worst of what Garcia had done.

In moving his herds to the north, he had squatted himself in the middle of another, completely legal land grant. James Berry had been granted a ranch which extended from Point Reyes to the mainland of the Marin Peninsula, a ranch which Garcia had now effectively divided into two unconnected pieces of land. One might think that this would have doomed Garcia's second petition; the local official, probably Timothy Murphy, at least would have noted the factual errors in Garcia's document. But this assumes that people were then careful about such things. Suffice it to say, Rafael Garcia received his second grant.

This bare fact would have been ominous in another context. James Berry had been unjustly deprived of thousands of acres of land; and the rest was greatly reduced in worth. He would seem to have no alternative except force.

But Berry was not a frontiersman carving out an existence in a hostile environment; he was a rancher living off the fat of the land. He did not want any trouble. He simply moved all his herds onto the Point Reyes portion of his land. Of course, this portion of his grant was too small for those herds. They now drifted onto Point Reyes land which had been granted to another rancher, Antonio Osio. (After Berry had gotten his grant, Osio had applied for Point Reyes Sobrante, literally, "Point Reyes Remaining," what was left of Point Reyes after Berry's grant.)

With Osio we have finally reached a rancher who was jealous of his property rights; but it seems to have made no difference. He had no more effective means of complaint against Berry's incursion than he did against the elk hunts which Garcia regularly conducted on the herds that fattened themselves on Osio's wild oats.

The simple fact was that there existed no effective unit of administration above the extended family of the ranch. The Mexican-supported military in California had declined from seven hundred to barely one hundred, and that included veterans who could only be called into service in an emergency. The cannons of the San Francisco fort had long been too decrepit to fire. The only effective law in a region like Marin was that created by a voluntary association of ranchers. There were certain simple rules governing the allocation of strays during round-up. There was little need for more. The bond between the ranchers was familial. Every ranch family was related to almost all surrounding families through marriage; at the least they shared in-laws. So when the ranching families came together, it was not to govern but only to celebrate, to celebrate their plenty.

These celebrations were conducted on a large scale; there would be parties for the whole region which would last for days. The daylight would be given to horse racing and other ranch sports; the night to singing and dancing. Eating and drinking would continue day and night. Memoirs of this period insist that there seemed to be always one such party somewhere in the bay region, and any rancher would be welcome.

The biggest such fiesta for the Marin Peninsula occurred each year during the week of the religious feast of Saint Raphael Archangel. This celebration, of course, was descended from mission days, when a solemn high mass would be offered for the angel of healing. But now the host was not the friar. Now he was Timothy Murphy, who put on a party equal to his size, he who towered as an archangel among men. And the ranchers had their own ritual, one that was not a celebration of a God who gives Himself to us in the agricultural products of bread and wine. Neither was it a reverent remembrance of an execution willed by the victim.

The central event of the new San Rafael Day was a fight to the death between a grizzly and a bull. These were, of course, two of the most powerful animals the ranchers knew: one the ranchers found here, the other they had introduced; one a meat-eater, the other a grazer; one a killer with claws and fangs, the other with horns and hooves. A bull and bear fight was the ritualized syzygy of the rancher's bloody cosmology.

The grizzly and the bull were yoked together with a rawhide rope. They could not escape one another, as ordinarily they probably would. (Of the full grown livestock, grizzlies usually only attacked horses.) Often the fight took time to start. The grizzly was frequently already fatigued from fighting his human captors. Nonetheless, once the fight began, the grizzly usually won. Sometimes it would mount the bull's back, sinking its claws into his flanks; in the bull's desperation to free himself, he would attempt to hook the grizzly with his horns, only thereby to bare his throat to the grizzly's jaws. Other times the grizzly would parry the bull until it could fix its jaws on the bull's lips or nose, and then it would hold on until the struggling bull had bled himself into exhaustion.

The bull's one chance was surprise, to gore the grizzly while it was still distracted by its noisy surroundings. Even then, the dying grizzly in its mortal rage would likely kill the bull before the end.

At first it might seem odd that the ranchers would take pleasure in a spectacle which consistently demonstrated the superiority of the grizzly over the protector of their herds. But the values this fight celebrated were quite different. It celebrated the superiority of the predator over his prey, of the flesh eater over the field grazer, of the hunter over the herd. (And so when the grizzlies became rare on the peninsula near the end of the ranch era, and had to be replaced, they were replaced by a man; the unwilling bull was now to be sacrificed by a matador.)

Of course, the primitiveness of these celebrations did not pass unnoticed by those who visited California from the larger world. "As I sat in a house of antique construction, looked upon the primitive manners of the Father, the unaffected hospitality of our hostess, and the convivial hilarity of all, feudal recollections passed rapidly through my mind. I felt myself transported back to former centuries and mingling in the transactions of an age that is past."

This was written by a visitor to John Reed's ranch in the late 1830s. The visitor had enjoyed his stay, but only as a visitor. He had no desire to reside in an age that was past. The discomfort of such a life, as much as anything, weighed against it. For instance, this particular guest had arrived at the Reed lands at low tide. Hence to reach Reed's house he had to find his way through miles of tidal marsh. The way of life was quaint, but not enviable.

John Reed himself, if we are to believe the account of another visitor, was disgusted with it. Duflot du Mofrat, who claimed to know Reed well, wrote that Reed had become so discouraged by all his hardships that he would like nothing better than to sell his herds and leave California altogether. Whether or not this is accurate, Reed's life does evidence one of the many drawbacks of California ranch life.

In 1838 John Reed fell from his horse, an apparent victim of sunstroke. Since there was no doctor within riding distance, his friends gathered to do what they could to help the prostrate Reed regain his strength. They decided to bleed him. From their ranch experience they found it easy enough to open his veins. However, having done so, they found themselves unequal to the task of closing the veins back up again. This at least is one account of how otherwise healthy, thirty-eight-year-old John Reed died from sunstroke. He bled to death.

It was against the day to day discomforts which most travelers rebelled. The California rancher was hospitable to a fault; he would

give you anything he had. But in many ways he had little to give. The
ranchers, as a group, did not know how to work wood; some made
fences for their vegetable gardens out of stacked cattle skulls. Only
the wealthiest ranchers had any furniture. At most ranches everyone would simply sit on the dirt floor; some ranchers near the coast
had taken to using pieces of whale bone for chairs. And if the average
rancher could not work wood, he certainly could not work metal.
Not even a wealthy rancher could be expected to provide utensils
with which to eat. The tortilla was the Californian's spoon and fork,
a new setting for every few bites. If a guest desired his meat in small
pieces, he was expected to bring his own knife.

Many found this coarseness of life hard to accept. Revere had
written, "Sentiment soon subsides on the hunting ground." But the
whole of California was now a hunting ground; and its society was a
society of hunters and butchers long inured to the sight of flowing
blood. One had to be accustomed to blood to enjoy the popular California sport of carrera de gallo. A chicken was buried up to its neck;
a horseman at a full gallop would attempt to pluck its head from its
shoulders, to leave but spurting blood in view of the cheering spec-
tators. It was a considerable feat of horsemanship, but difficult to
appreciate as such when first witnessed.

There was no formal education available on the Marin Peninsula or the rest of the bay region during the ranch period. Many of
the ranchers who held major Marin grants could neither read nor
write. Moreover, the common conversation, even between the sexes,
was sprinkled with what one traveler termed "gross expressions
and...broad remarks which would make modest women blush."
The travelers, especially the Americans, somehow could not quite
adjust to the fact that these people lived so close to their herds they
shared most things with them, including their parasites. "It is common to see them pick fleas and vermin off their persons....Indeed
the whole of California, including the towns, is a flea bitten country.
Ladies at parties, dressed in silks and satins, are often compelled to
clap their hands on their legs and pinch the little tormentor to
death."

The image of ladies in silks and satins pinching fleas to death
says much about California ranch life. The ranchers and their families loved to conspicuously display their few luxuries—party clothes
of silk and satin, saddles worked with silver and gold, all purchased
at great expense. These luxuries were so cherished precisely because

they were only a veneer. They no more represented the way of life than did the legal formalities of land acquisition. This was a society, not of silk or satin, but of rawhide. Rawhide was its chief manufactured item; it was the base on which all was built. And it was used for everything conceivable.

One California traveler wrote, "I had no idea of the many uses to which rawhides are put here. I was in a house on a ranch where rawhide was spread before the beds as carpet or mat. Bridle reins and ropes for lassos are made, fences are tied, everything is done with rawhide." He called rawhide the "universal plaster" of California ranch life.

That such a substance would be the universal plaster reveals the essential simplicity of the way of life it held together. And it was this simplicity that men like Lauff wished to remember, the simplicity, the happiness, the not worrying tomorrow. The routine of ranch life had created an illusion of timelessness, of the future being always like the past, of history, of time having stopped. Or so one of the old ranchers said.

"The sameness of recurring events of each succeeding year never seemed monotonous, but brought repose, contentment and peace. When the dew was still on the grass, we would mount our horses and herd the cattle if any had strayed beyond the pasture. In the wooded canyons where the cool brooks flowed, and where the wild blackberries grew, we ate our noon day meal and rested. And as the hills began to glow with the light of the setting sun we journeyed homeward.... Those were days long ago. Now all is changed by modern progress, but in the simple ranch life of the older time there was a contented happiness which an alien race with different temperament can never understand."

The rancher's control of his world was based upon rawhide. With rawhide rope the rancher caught and broke a horse. Rawhide reins gave him control of the horse. A rawhide saddle held him on the horse's back. And from there he could dominate the range life. Not the man alone, but the horseman, was the predator which could outmaneuver the grizzly bear, and begin its extermination.

Yet to maintain his way of life the rancher had to permit the intrusion of another alien race of predators, or what seemed at times to be such. California was virtually devoid of industry; almost any manufactured item in California, except for that made of adobe, rawhide, and the like, had to be imported and bartered in exchange for hides and tallow. This included all cloth, from cottons to silk, all hardware from needles to spades; it included thread, glass, even good leather, perhaps made originally from a California cowhide.

The alien race with a different temperament who exchanged these items for the "California banknote" (as they called the hide) were the Yankee seaman merchants. The California hide and tallow trade was dominated by essentially the same merchant fleet that had skinned the California coast of its fur bearing animals a decade or two earlier. Now the Yankees settled for a less glamorous trade, but one of considerable size and steadiness. By the late 1830s the Yankees were taking hundreds of thousands of hides and thousands of tons of tallow out of California each year. It has been estimated that the average ranching family was annually exporting more than four hundred hides and more than ten tons of tallow.

The Mexican government was an impediment to this trade. Quite understandably, Mexico had endeavored to protect its own infant industries by placing prohibitive tariffs on competing foreign goods. However, these industries had not developed sufficiently to supply their products to its remote province of California. Nonetheless, the prohibitive tariffs remained in effect there, although the Mexican government was almost powerless to enforce them.

This lack of an effective central authority meant that the Yankees themselves could not be regulated. And they gradually recognized the strength of their position. The California herds were becoming so large that the ranchers, to prevent overgrazing, had to slaughter a sizable portion each year, as much as a third; the Yankees were the only ones to whom they could sell the resultant hides and tallow; and the Yankees were the only ones supplying them with the cherished luxuries on which their social position seemed to depend. Inevitably, the Yankees began to behave like the monopolists they were. Profits of one hundred percent had been routine; now profits of three to four hundred percent were not unusual.

Some of the north bay ranchers attempted to lessen the economic pressure by diversifying their production, by becoming farmers as well as ranchers. This effort was thwarted when Yankees simply refused to trade for any surplus except hides and tallow. In 1844 Mariano Vallejo wrote a grim assessment of the situation to the Mexican government.

Foreign hunters had already destroyed one of California's great natural resources—its population of fur bearing animals. Now foreign merchants were causing the destruction of its other great source of wealth—its ranches. "Besides charging prices so exorbitant as to be fradulent, they are standing together in accepting only hides and tallow, and no agricultural products. Thus it is that the rancher does not cultivate his fields, and the stock is diminishing." Vallejo wished the Mexican government to realize that the California ranchers were no longer masters of their own way of life. It was slowly being strangled by these outsiders. Vallejo pleaded with Mexico for help, but privately knew better than to expect any.

The frustration the Californians felt at being caught between exorbitant tariffs and outrageous profits is aptly expressed in a change in the common name by which the Californians of European origin referred to themselves. In the Spanish and early Mexican period they had referred to themselves as the "race of reason," to distinguish themselves from the California Indians. Now they assumed a name which could be equally shared by those Indians—indeed, which was more rightly theirs. The California ranchers now preferred to call themselves "the native sons and daughters." They, like the Indians, were of this place. And this fact distinguished them from outsiders like the Yankees.

If ranch life was being strangled from the outside, it was also dying from within. More than they needed the Yankee traders, the ranchers needed the Indian laborers. And the Indians were dying out.

This particular danger had been with the ranchers from the beginning. The first major smallpox epidemic swept the north bay region in 1835; by some estimates tens of thousands of Indians were killed. At San Rafael the Indians had to be buried in mass graves. Vallejo's whole design for the development of the region was threatened by depopulation of the laboring class.

Perhaps it is not a coincidence that 1835 was the year Vallejo organized his expedition against hostile tribes to the north, far enough north that they might have been spared the smallpox. Thus, after the battle and subsequent atrocities, Vallejo divided up the surviving captives among the Europeans who had participated. There were about one hundred captives, including sixty-five "bucks" as the mature males were called.

This was obviously at best a temporary measure, and one which set a dangerous precedent. Vallejo had pacified the north bay region by helping friendly tribes settle traditional grudges against their neighbors. Vallejo did not mind enslaving a tribe which was a traditional enemy of Stone Hands and other Indian allies. However, if such methods began to be used on tribes which had made peace with the Europeans, the ranchers and Vallejo with them might face a general uprising that could sweep away all that they had built.

Twice during the five years after his northern raid Vallejo had to break up north bay kidnapping rings which sold to ranchers children stolen from friendly but still free tribes. One of these rings had been led by none other than Vallejo's most important Indian ally, Stone Hands; of the children he and his ring had sold, Vallejo was able to return about thirty to their parents.

The ranchers, however, could do little. The epidemics continued to recur every few years during the 1840s. Sometimes it was measles, sometimes smallpox; but the result was the same. (During one smallpox epidemic of the 1840s, Chief Stone Hands' own tribe was almost entirely wiped out. Stone Hands would survive, but was now largely stripped of his power. When he eventually died, Vallejo had to hide his grave within the intricate network of North Bay sloughs. Even so, his enemies claimed to have found it within twenty-four hours, and to have treated his body to the indignities the living man had deserved.) As one rancher put it, "The Indians who were taught by the Spanish Padres the different Mechanical Arts are now dead, and no more of their tribe will ever take their place." A rancher was now faced with the choice between doing more and more of the skilled work himself, or paying another European to do it for him. The times were changing, and everyone who understood was beginning to worry tomorrow.

Even the range was changing for the worse, although this was harder to see. There was, of course, danger of overgrazing now. And the cattle herds were starting to press against the game. The deer could retreat to the hills, but the elk and antelope herds drifted to the north, off the peninsula for good. And if the cattle had not forced them out, then the grasses would have. Native California grasses were quickly being replaced by European grasses, the seeds of which were presumably carried to the New World by the livestock. The native range plants were no more equipped to survive European competition than were the native range animals.

The native California grasses were, for the most part, perennials. They would survive the arid summers by drying out except for a small green portion near the ground. The Mediterranean grasses had evolved a more efficient means of species survival. They were annuals, dying each summer to be reborn through their seeds when the rain came again.

A herd placed on a summer field of both European annuals and California perennials would tend to overgraze on the still partly green California grasses. When such overgrazing was done by the large herds the ranchers now introduced onto the range, the California grasses were gradually exterminated in favor of the less palatable European grasses.

But the European grasses were not only less palatable to grazers; they were also less nourishing. They tend to produce indigestible seeds. Hence a grazer that swallows such a seed will probably pass it unharmed, and it will await the rains in a heap of manure. It is a wonderful mechanism for the preservation of heavily-grazed grass, but a poor one for the sustenance of a grazer.

To Joseph Revere's eyes the wild oats on which the elk had gorged themselves must have seemed as much a native son of the California range as were the elk. But this was a European plant. The elk had to gorge on it because it did not provide them with continuous forage; once it died, they were faced with hard times. The smaller, "rangy" Mexican cattle were well adapted to this; for centuries their ancestors had foraged on such land in Europe. For the bulky elk it was yet another unprecedented trial.

Revere might have suspected that elk could not long survive such hunts as the one he had enjoyed. But he must have assumed that these harmless wild oats, would still be there in fifty years, still dominating the range. Yet nature has a slow logic of its own. Species rise, thrive, and decline, much as do the human societies that live off them. The wild oat, and the grasses associated with it, had proven hardier than the native grasses. And so it supplanted them. The native grasses found themselves pushed to the fringes of the range, there to survive as best they could, never again to flourish.

But the oats were as subject to nature's phases as were the California grasses. Soon the oats with their allied grasses were being challenged by another group of European grasses, prominent among them wild barley. These grasses were hardier than the oats, and even worse forage. And eventually even the introduced barleys would be challenged in parts of the California range by a group of grasses more competitive still. The names given some of these grasses imply what impossible forage they are, goatgrass, dogtail, cat's ear. It was as if a forager would have to eat fur.

One of this last group, a wild rye is perhaps the most feared by those ranchers who still today live off herds that live off the range. If it is present on a range, one sees it best after the dry season has killed the less tenacious annuals. This rye will still be green. Each plant will have a large head of indigestible seeds—it is almost all seeds and no leaf—a head which will look down upon the dead grasses around it. This wild rye is called Medusa Head; and it, unless fought, will kill a range, making it little better than stone.

Of course, the California ranchers of the Mexican period saw only the beginning of this change in the grasses—and even then could not have understood its implications for the future. For them the forage of the range seemed timeless, affected only by the cyclical rhythms of the weather. But that did not matter, for they had begun to see time elsewhere. They saw their society progressively being destroyed from without and decaying from within.

Some of the most perceptive of these Californians, like Vallejo, occasionally used a phrase to sum up their deteriorating situation, a phrase which starkly contrasts with "the fat of the land." The phrase evokes—for someone familiar with California life in this period—a moment in an elk hunt, the moment when the elk realize that they are trapped, trapped between their predators and perhaps cliffs falling off to the sea. The California ranchers had begun to recognize around themselves a "closing circle of peril."

In retrospect, the ranch society seems to have been doomed from the beginning. The idyll was an illusion. The apparently secure foundations of ranch life were actually, when examined closely, slowly shifting toward its destruction. What seemed a timeless thing to those that built it was only a passing shadow on the land, a shadow that would disappear in less than a human lifetime.

Perhaps the Marin ranchers knew this all along, in a way. Perhaps they knew it when they thought about the bone-dotted fields, or the crescent gleam of the luna, or the grizzly's breath. They might not have wished to remember it as old men, but they had their glimpses of this empty truth even in their prime. One of their tall tales said as much, in its way.

The story was told of Thomas Wood, a deserter from a ship on the Marin coast in the 1830s. Wood settled with an Indian woman and her people near Tomales Bay (the loch behind the coyote's ear), an unusual decision in this period. Although he stood aloof and refused to sign on as a permanent hand for any ranch, he was soon reputed to be the best horseman on the peninsula and the best with a riata.

Tom Vaquero, he came to be called, Cowboy Tom. Timothy Murphy may have been the host of San Rafael Day, but Tom Vaquero was its star. He had one standing challenge that, as far as is known, no one ever successfully accepted. Tom Vaquero could break any wild horse of the peninsula on the first try. More than that, he could break any horse while keeping a silver dollar pressed in each of his stirrups. Far from being able to throw him, no horse could even loosen one of his feet from its stirrup. This was Tom Vaquero, quintessence of the California horseman.

One day Tom Vaquero, as the story was to be told, came across a grizzly bear peacefully grazing on clover in the middle of a field. Everyone knew how two skilled horsemen could take a grizzly alive with their riatas. They would approach the bear from opposite sides. When the bear charged one, the other would lasso its back legs and throw it. Before the bear could regain its balance the second horseman would place his rope around the front legs. Hopelessly enmeshed in rawhide, the grizzly would soon find itself being taken back to a ranch for an encounter with a bull.

With two skilled horsemen a grizzly bear could be taken easily. But Tom Vaquero on this fated day had no one with him. He and the grizzly confronted each other alone, except for the horse and riata Tom had for help. No one had ever taken a grizzly with so little; it was too formidable a feat even to try. Nonetheless, Tom was the very best vaquero that had ever been on the peninsula; his riata was a good one; and his horse was a "thoroughly trained lass animal." If anyone could do it, he could do it now. Tom Vaquero decided that he was "entirely master of the situation, and concluded to try to take the bear home."

"With riata gyrating over his head, he swooped down upon bruin, and with unerring precision hurled the noose around the bear's neck." The other end of the riata he wrapped around his saddle horn. Then he began to drive and to drag the grizzly the miles toward his home, the hundred feet of the riata giving the horseman ample room to maneuver.

The struggle was difficult. For at least an hour Tom and his horse held the grizzly on their leash. The horseman seemed clearly the master of the situation.

Finally he had reached within view of his home; one-half mile more to go, and bruin would never again taste clover or flesh. But Tom's home was on the shore of the bay, the building itself being constructed from wreckage salvaged from the sea.

As his horse tried to close the final distance to the sea wreck Tom called home, the footing gradually worsened. Soon the horse's hooves were sinking deep into sand. This soft terrain made the bear's strength more than a match for the horseman's agility. And the grizzly seemed to realize that its time had come at last.

The grizzly was now the predator, the horseman the prey. The best the horseman could do was to elude its ferocious charges. And at this very moment, in the fright of this unexpected reversal, Tom Vaquero was betrayed by his riata. The rawhide riata became tangled in the saddle; Tom somehow could not free it.

But this was not as extraordinary as the behavior of the bear, once it realized Tom was no longer master of his own riata. If we are to believe the story, the grizzly began to act like more than a bear. It became calm, and ceased its charges. Instead the grizzly simply "sat down on his haunches and methodically commenced taking in the slack of the riata with his paws, as a man would a rope, hand-over-hand."

This reversal was so great, such a violation of the accustomed order of things, that Tom could not think. He seemed fascinated by the image of a grizzly using a riata to take a horseman. Half of the riata's length had been taken in before he recovered his presence of mind. Then he was close enough to look the bear in the face, and to "see deliberate murder in the grizzly's eyes." This meeting of eyes brought Thomas Wood back to his senses. He remembered he had a knife, and "with it succeeded in severing the wiry raw-hide coil which had fouled on the horn of the saddle."

Freed at last, Thomas Wood had no hesitation about what he should do next. "He beat a hasty retreat, leaving the bear victor of the field and winner of a riata worth at that time not less than ten dollars."

Bear and vaquero
Courtesy of the Bancroft Library

A Marin Ranch
Courtesy of the Bancroft Library

VI
The Bear's Flag

James Miller, with his wife and children (one an infant), arrived on the Marin Peninsula in April, 1845. He soon found employment with Juan Cooper, who owned a large tract of land south of San Rafael but preferred to live in Monterey. Cooper had chosen this land for its redwood forest, and now he permitted James Miller to lumber it provided they shared the proceeds equally. Within a year Miller had made enough money from his lumbering to buy eight hundred acres of his own, on the plains to the north of San Rafael. Over the next few decades he expanded his holdings until by 1880 he owned more than eight thousand acres, and Miller House itself was a showplace of the peninsula.

There is nothing particularly notable about the success story of James Miller—except, that is, the adventure that preceded it, and made it possible. Miller and his family had arrived in California from the east, by land. They had been members of the first wagon train that successfully crossed the dark and deathlike wall of the Sierra Nevada.

This wagon train set out from Council Bluffs, Iowa, in May of 1844. Miller and his wife and her extensive family, the Murphys, had settled earlier in Missouri, but a malaria epidemic had killed four of them. The Murphys decided to move on. Of the eleven wagons that left Council Bluffs for California that May, five were owned by relatives, either direct or through marriage, of Mrs. Miller.

By July 4, 1844, the Millers' wagon train had reached Independence Rock in what is now Wyoming. Here the Millers and Murphys had a good omen. Miller's wife had left Iowa knowing she was pregnant. This day she gave birth to a healthy baby girl, whom the parents named Mary Independence in honor of the occasion.

111

By mid-August the Murphys and other prospective Californians had left the Oregon trail to seek California. The next month or two of travel was uneventful. As one of the memoirs puts it, "The journey down the Humboldt was very monotonous. Each day's events were substantially a repetition of those of the day before." But this monotony was preferable to the confrontation with the Sierra Nevada that began in October.

Only two other wagon trains had attempted to overcome the Sierra Nevada, one in 1841, the other in 1843. They both tried to skirt the mountains to the south. This required a long journey down the barren eastern side of the mountain chain that put a great strain on supplies and endurance. In fact, this strain had proven too great for those two earlier wagon trains which had been forced to abandon their wagons in order to reach California safely.

The only alternative to running south was to attempt a direct western thrust in the hope of finding a pass through the heart of the mountains. People who had already left the more secure route to Oregon might be expected to be gamblers at heart; but the Sierra Nevada was an awesome sight. The Millers' train hesitated on the decision until what appeared to be a piece of good luck decided the matter.

An old Indian called Truckee, was found, who told through sign language of a river with banks of pasture that flowed from the mountains. A scouting party found that Truckee had told the truth. So the wagons started west along the river they named the Truckee in his honor. Truckee had told the truth as far as he knew it, but the wagons were not long in coming to other truths. The river banks which were at first pleasant meadows eventually became canyon walls. The animals and men had to spend more and more time each day in the freezing water, so much time that the hooves of animals began to soften. Then, to make matters worse, the first snows fell, burying the grass. The men tried to feed the animals pine needles, with little success. The animals were so weakened that when they did come across a patch of tules growing up through the snow two died from gorging themselves.

By November 14 the now weakened party had reached a fork in both the river and its canyon. Once again they were given the choice between a direct but difficult route west and an easier but longer route to the south. And once again they chose to go directly west, but now they began to hedge their bets. Four men and two women were outfitted with horses and supplies, and sent on the southern route. Perhaps this more quickly moving group would reach California sooner, and send back help.

The wagons had moved only a few more miles when they were faced with a ridge with no apparent pass. After some exploration, the group decided that six of the wagons should be left behind here, three of the younger men volunteering to remain with them through the winter to protect the goods from the Indians. Nonetheless, even this compromise did not appear enough. The five remaining wagons, as they struggled up the granite ridge, were suddenly stopped, finally it seemed, by a ten foot vertical face which could not be avoided. But at this point the leader of the expedition, at least as he later recounted the crisis, prayed to God for guidance, and was granted a vision showing him exactly how he could surmount the obstacle. So the train moved on.

By the time the wagons began their descent down the western side of the mountains winter had undeniably come; the snow had reached four feet. For three days they attempted to break into easier country, only to be confronted at each crest with canyons and ridges, more canyons and ridges. And in the midst of this effort they had to pause to let another baby be born. Finally, early in December, the decision was made that a winter camp had to be formed for the women and children. A cabin was built, and what remained of the cattle they had driven with them for food was slaughtered. Then seventeen of the nineteen men pushed on by horseback toward California, promising to return with help as early as possible in the spring. Of the two men who remained, one was an old man too weak to continue, the other was James Miller. By late February people in the cabin had been reduced to eating hides, but by then the snows had eased. James Miller set off with a young son toward California; on his way he met the first of those coming with relief.

"We find ourselves suddenly threatened by hordes of Yankee emigrants, who have already begun to flock into our country, and whose progress we cannot arrest. Already have wagons of that perfidious people scaled the almost inaccessible summits of the Sierra Nevada, crossed the entire continent, and penetrated the fruitful valley of the Sacramento. . . . What are we to do? Shall we remain supine, while these daring strangers are overrunning our fertile plains, and gradually outnumbering and displacing us? Shall these incursions go on unchecked, until we become strangers in our own land?"

This is from a speech attributed to Pio Pico, the governor of California, only two years after the Millers left Council Bluffs. The California trail was now open, and Pio Pico saw the threat clearly. In this very speech he complained that the Mexican settlers had never been able to fully exploit the blessings of California because their population had been too sparse. And this sparsity could not be denied. By 1846, the year of this speech, the European population of the whole province of California had yet to reach five thousand. (On the Marin Peninsula the Europeans still numbered no more than a few dozen.) What made Pio Pico sensitive to this deficiency was not this population considered in itself, for the ranch society was based upon a disparity between the small number of European landowners and the large, if now decreasing, number of available Indian laborers. Rather, it was the population of California compared to the population of millions that had made the United States a westwardly expanding power. (Just the European immigration into the United States alone was more than a million a year.) Already the Hispanic population in Texas had been swamped, and Texas was now the newest state in the Union. For a time California seemed preserved from such a fate by the granite wall of the Sierra Nevada—let the Yankees have Oregon. But now that the wall had been breeched, the danger was present and increasing. And Pio Pico could foresee the end: he and his people would share the fate they had imposed upon the Indians, to be strangers in their own land.

There had been an earlier, smaller, and therefore less threatening Yankee immigration into California. Juan Cooper, who gave James Miller his start on the Marin Peninsula, was typical of this earlier group. John Cooper, as he was then known, arrived at Monterey in the 1820s on his own ship, out of Boston. Realizing that fur trading was illegal, Cooper had entered into a partnership with the governor of California, and subsequently his trading efforts went unnoticed. By the 1840s Juan Cooper had converted to Roman Catholicism, become a Mexican citizen, married a sister of Mariano Vallejo, and been granted two large pieces of land on the Marin Peninsula, one of them half of Nicasio.

The Yankees, like Cooper, who arrived in California for maritime commerce worked within the society as they found it. They

were indistinguishable from the northern European settlers like
Timothy Murphy. They had much more in common with these men,
or for that matter with the Hispanic Californians whose daughters
and sisters they married, than they did with the Yankees who began
wandering through California in the 1830s. These were the mountain men who, especially as guides, would eventually play an important role in the coming of the wagon trains.

Beaver fur was for a short time the landlubber equivalent of the
sea otter pelt. Fashionable European and American men of the
1830s required beaver fur hats much as Chinese courtiers still
required sea otter fringes. Yet for all the obvious parallels between
the sea otter trade and the beaver trade, the typical man produced
by each was quite different.

The Yankees who put to sea had to submit to, or to enforce,
the discipline of the ship. The hierarchy of command was definite;
floggings or worse awaited those who defied it. A John Cooper was
a man of order and command who would find his way to a comfortable position in almost any society in which he found himself. The
mountain men were of a different cast.

The land they faced was often as uncertain and treacherous
as the sea, but they faced it more as individuals than as groups. They
valued their liberty—their freedom from social restraint—at times
more than life itself. Their groups were less crews than bands; their
leaders less captains than chiefs. Moreover, the land's principle
danger, unlike the sea's, was human. In their wandering search for
beaver the mountain men were forever trespassing on the territory
of Indians, and poaching upon their hunting grounds. As a matter of
self-preservation, most mountain men became inured to the taking
of human life, and some clearly relished it.

One who clearly relished it, and perhaps the most famous of
mountain men, Kit Carson, told a story of visiting San Rafael during
the mission period. After spending the night at the mission, the
mountain men discovered some of their horses missing. According
to Carson, they tracked the thieves more than one hundred miles,
to within sight of the Sierra Nevada, before they came across fifty
Indians feasting on horsemeat. Unobserved, the mountain men surrounded the Indians, and had them at their mercy. But mountain
men, unlike ranchers, had no use for Indians, except to make lessons
of them. So they killed forty-nine, leaving one alive (although
wounded) so that he could tell the tale. Indians in these parts would

now know better than to take trappers' horses.

For Kit Carson homicide was clearly more than just an occupational necessity. He liked to tell the tale, for instance, of the time he mistakenly tried to scalp an Indian not quite dead. (Carson regularly took scalps.) He wasn't more than half through when the Indian stood up, and started staggering around. Carson was so surprised he couldn't move, and someone else had to shoot the Indian again before Carson could finish the job. What made the whole incident even more comical was that it all took place in front of a wailing old woman whom Carson took to be the boy's mother.

By the 1840s men like Kit Carson were having to look beyond trapping for their livelihood. By then the beaver fur trade was in decline, never truly to revive. (Modish men now required felt hats.) However, the mountain men had in their unsystematic way explored much of the land—and fought most of the Indians—between the United States and the Pacific Coast. These services proved indispensible to Americans like the Millers who wished to move west.

So the Millers' success as Californians had depended upon both groups of Americans who had preceded them. The mountain men had facilitated their passage; and, once arrived, they found that one of the maritime traders, Juan Cooper, would help them get established. However, in the latter assistance they were not just fortunate, but also untypical.

Most of the early American immigrants felt that *they* were the strangers in a strange land. Unlike Cooper and Miller, but like the mountain men, they did not wish to become part of this alien society. Most chose to remain away from the coast, many congregating in the Sacramento Valley Pio Pico had specifically mentioned in his speech. There they were perhaps more vulnerable to hostile Indian attack, but there also they would be far removed from the influence, weak as it was, of the Mexican government. There they could wait while each year their numbers increased. And they, as well as the California governor, knew what these numbers meant. The numbers brought closer the day California would be ruled by the United States; the immigrants had only to hold out until they were strong enough.

While they waited, they could not but be encouraged by the historical myth that was gaining currency in the country they still regarded as their own, the myth of manifest destiny. The United States had a manifest destiny, ordained by providence, to rule from the Atlantic to the Pacific, and perhaps also from the Arctic Circle to the Panama Isthmus. This was a commonplace view in the land from which the wagon trains issued.

"Away, away with all these cobweb issues of rights of discovery, exploration, settlement, contiguity, etc.... [The claim of the United States] is by right of our manifest destiny to over spread and to possess the whole of the continent which Providence has given us for the development of the great experiment of liberty and federative self-government entrusted to us. It is a right such as that of the tree to the space of air and earth suitable for the full expansion of its principle and destiny of growth—such as that of the stream to the channel required for the still accumulating volume of its flow. It is in our future far more than in our past, or in the past history of Spanish exploration or French colonial rights, that our True Title is to be found."

These were the words of John L. O'Sullivan, advocate of manifest destiny, a Kit Carson of journalism. When the United States government finally decided in 1845 to annex the ex-Mexican province of Texas, O'Sullivan was little less than gleeful: "Texas, we repeat, is secure; and so now, as the Razor Strop Man says, 'Who's the next customer?' Shall it be California or Canada?"

John Fremont was betting on California. The written orders for his third exploratory expedition for the United States Topographical Engineers mentioned nothing about crossing the Sierra Nevada. But Fremont was, as he thought all could see, a man of destiny who did not permit himself to be limited by such trivial things as written orders. And, anyway, he could always claim, if challenged, that there were secret, oral orders which superceded the written, a ploy he had used before.

Fremont combined in his person the worst elements of the mountain man with those of the manifest destiny journalist. With the mountain men who guided him, notably Kit Carson, Fremont joined in the slaughter of Indians. The largest massacre of this particular expedition, for instance, would be that of a California village of about one hundred seventy-five, a massacre so bloody that Carson exulted in it as a "perfect butchery." Fremont at times would risk his whole expedition to engage Indians about whom he had suspicions.

But Fremont did not just participate in such atrocities; he glorified them. With the help of his wife (daughter of Thomas Hart

Benton, perhaps the most powerful expansionist in the United States
Senate), Fremont wrote accounts of his expeditions that were virtual
best sellers. In Fremont's purple prose (still imitated by his biog-
raphers) Kit Carson and his other mountain men became heroes of
the American frontier; and the Indians became the most dangerous
game, more difficult to take than even the bear.

"An Indian let loose is of all animals the most savage. He has
an imagination for devilment that seems peculiar to him, and singular delight in inflicting suffering." Such a description of the Indian
made the sadistic devilments of his own men achievements worthy
of the highest praise, praise which lesser men were not wont to give.
"Indian fighting, which calls for the utmost skill and courage on the
part of men, is not appreciated by the Government, or held worthy
of the notice given to the milder civilized warfare." The fact that a
heavily armed party such as his would inflict hundreds of casual-
ties for every one received only showed the skill and courage with
which Fremont led his men.

Fremont's mapping expedition, with Kit Carson as its chief
mountain man, dragging with it a piece of artillery (taken against
orders), arrived in California in 1846. Fremont knew that war between the United States and Mexico over Texas seemed imminent.
He also knew that California was, by many accounts, ripe for the
taking by any power daring enough to act. He only waited for the
opportunity to dare.

Fremont and his men were not long in California before they
were in difficulty with the Mexican authorities. They were accused
of stealing a horse. To the polite inquiry from a Mexican official
Fremont responded that the accuser had come to him with his claim
to own the horse, but the claim was false, and the man lucky to have
escaped without "a severe horsewhipping." And that was to be the
end of the matter. "You will readily understand that my duties will
not permit me to appear before the magistrates of your towns on the
complaint of every straggling vagabond who may chance to visit my
camp."

In this way Fremont managed to transform a trivial matter of
a horse into a potential international incident. The military commander at Monterey was now involved. Since Fremont was in California illegally in the first place and had subsequently defied local
authority, he was ordered to leave the territory. Fremont found that
order an offense to the honor of both his country and himself, and

he also thought the lieutenant who brought it did not show due respect. He pulled his men together on high ground, fortified it, raised the American flag, and waited for the war to begin.

Jose Castro, Mariano Vallejo's successor as commander of the northern frontier in California, wished only to save a little face. What claimed to be an official exploratory expedition of the United States government (but did not look like one) had openly defied the authority of his government. Then, when he ordered them out of his territory, they had fortified themselves on a hill, raised the American flag, and thumbed their collective nose. Now Castro had to find a peaceful way out of this awkward situation, one that would not embarrass him before his fellow Californians.

Even without these Americans flying their flag from a worthless hill, Castro had complications enough. The whole province of California had been in *de facto* revolt from Mexico since the previous year. The Mexican appointed governor, after a battle between his loyal troops and the native sons, had been sent back to Mexico wounded. The Mexican government might have been expected to take retaliatory action before now, had Mexico not been on the verge of war with the United States over Texas boundaries. And what implications a war between these two countries had for California no one knew. And, if all this were not enough, the new governor of California, who, as a native son, should have been popular throughout the province, had chosen to behave arbitrarily. He had decided to move the capital from Monterey, where it had always been, to southern California—closer to his ranch and family. Now northern California defied *his* authority, and in a California civil war Castro would be the leader of the northern troops.

The situation was undeniably—almost unbelievably—complex. Mexico seemed close to war with the United States; California had revolted against Mexico; northern California was defiant of the rest of California. And now, in the midst of all this, to complete the circle, an official expedition of the United States government tries to start a war between the United States and northern California. Mariano Vallejo at Sonoma was to be envied in his retirement; but Jose Castro at Monterey was going to have to do the best he could.

The Americans were inviting battle, an invitation Castro could neither accept nor decline. Castro did make preparations for a great battle, and beligerently moved his collected troops this way and that. He did not attack, however, and carefully left open a north-ward escape route for the Americans to use, once they realized that the threatened attack would never come. It could have been a dis-creet victory if only the Americans had not been so pointedly slow when they finally did begin to move. (They moved north, Fremont would write, "slowly and growlingly.")

Castro only wanted to preserve his forces for future contingen-cies. If some around him thought his inaction a sign of weakness, he would reassure them by fulminating against Americans generally, and threatening expulsion to all those who had illegally entered the area of his command. And he would also use this incident as an ex-cuse to round up government horses north of the bay, in particular those kept at Mission San Rafael. To drive them around the bay to the south took time; Castro would have it done now so that they would be at hand for an emergency. In all this Castro had done nothing unreasonable, but it made no difference. The complexity of the circumstances was about to undo him.

Castro's threats against Americans became larger, more im-mediate, more literal as they were carried north. Even Indians who stole horses for food were perceived by the more excitable Ameri-cans as conspirators in a grand Mexican strategy against them. And the mysterious reappearance of the exploratory party increased the excitement. Fremont and his men had almost reached Oregon when they were intercepted (it was said) by a secret agent from the Ameri-can government; they then returned with him to California. The Mexicans apparently were not the only ones plotting, although Fremont was saying nothing.

Frightened by one unexpected event and emboldened by another, the American immigrants then learned of the horses being driven from San Rafael to Monterey. Obviously this was a part of the Mexican plot against them, whatever it was; they would become an active part of the American plot for them, whatever it was.

Lieutenant Francisco Arce must have been more than a little bewildered when he discovered that he was surrounded. He was aware of California's complex position in world affairs. He even likened her position to that of a beautiful girl whom everyone wanted. But all that had nothing to do with his present task, which was simply to herd some government horses from one place to another. Nothing could have seemed more routine, and if Castro had thought there was any chance of trouble, he would have given him more than two men.

The fact, however, was indisputable. He was surrounded and outnumbered. So he did the only reasonable thing: he surrendered. There was no point in getting oneself killed for some horses. Nonetheless, Arce did, at least according to one account, decide to make a small gesture to Honor: after he was safely in the capture of the Americans, he is supposed to have said that if the Americans had not surprised him and his men, they would have gladly fought to the death.

Arce, like Castro, had not reckoned on the literal minds of the Americans. The leader of the group which had attacked Arce was a mountain man, Ezekiel Merritt. "Stuttering Merritt," as he was known, neither spoke nor thought without obvious difficulty. As near as Merritt could tell, the greaser had said it hadn't been a fair fight. Well, nobody could say that Zeke Merritt didn't fight fair. He offered to have his men ride out of the camp, to let the Mexicans get as ready as they liked, and then to come back to take the horses from them again, this time over their dead bodies.

Whether "Stuttering Merritt" was amused, annoyed, or just plain perplexed when Lieutenant Arce respectfully declined his gracious offer was not recorded. What was recorded was that Zeke let Arce and his men ride off to tell Castro that if he wanted his horses back, he should come and try to take them. Jose Castro was now to have more to worry about than his horses, or even his face.

The next Mexican leader to have an encounter with Zeke Merritt and his growing band was Mariano Vallejo himself. Early one morning Vallejo found himself surrounded and still in his nightshirt. He had no more expected an attack on Sonoma than Arce had expected a raid on his horses. Vallejo was a retired commander, openly friendly to Americans; his town was no longer an official garrison.

Vallejo treated the Americans as he might have treated renegade Indians. He met them in friendship, invited their leaders into private conference, and then opened a bottle or two of his best brandy. As Vallejo must have expected, Stuttering Merritt and the other leaders did not know exactly what they wanted from him. And so the negotiations continued, while Vallejo conceded more and more of his brandy.

Vallejo, however, did not reckon on Benjamin Ide—or so Ide

claimed in his memoirs. Ide, then in his fifties, was the oldest of the rebels; more importantly, he was a teetotaler. This did not endear him to his fellow Americans, who suspected him of being a "Mormon." But when the men left outside in the morning cold began to suspect what was happening in the negotiations, and particularly after the first person they sent to find out what was happening failed to return, Ide's strange temperance was a strong recommendation.

And so it was, at least by Ide's own account, that he saved the revolution. When he entered Vallejo's house, he discovered Merritt and the rest almost speechless with brandy. Under Ide's direction the flow of brandy stopped. Vallejo was declared a prisoner of war, to be sent under guard further behind the lines. California was to be a republic, and "Mormon" Ide its Washington.

Ide supplied the rebels with a fine sounding proclamation calling all Americans, and others of good will, to their standard in the name of liberty, justice, and the like. Of course, there needed to be a flag flying from the standard. They easily settled on the central object for this flag, a grizzly bear. They saw themselves as grizzlies rampaging for liberty. And the name, in a way, stuck. Their revolt has come to be known as the Bear Flag Revolt, and they simply as the Bears.

The execution of the Bear Flag itself was not so easy. The artist, whatever his talents, was working under extreme limitations. According to one account, he had to paint the grizzly with berry juice. Not surprisingly, he did not achieve a good likeness. In fact, to some eyes, the rampaging grizzly bore a remarkable resemblance to a rooting hog.

The hog-bear was not enough for the flag. There was added a red star and stripe. The red flannel cloth used in this step became later an object of controversy. Two wives of bears each claimed that the flannel was torn exclusively from her petticoat. Benjamin Ide, with his sense of decorum, distinctly remembered that the red flannel had come from a man's shirt.

This still was not enough. Although it was a flag, few people would know what it was a flag of. So, "California Republic" was to be written under the bear. This presented its own difficulty. In the first rendering "republic" was misspelt; and, although this was corrected, signs of the mistake remained. (These signs would subsequently be the sure test used to distinguish the first bear flag from later copies.)

And so there was founded in Sonoma, in 1846, a new republic—the misspelt, red flannel republic of Porky the Bear.

Now that his republic had a flag and a proclamation, Ide sent out messengers to rally Americans to its cause, and also to get more powder. Many Americans now felt compelled to join the rebellion. One of them later explained that he knew the revolt against the Mexicans was unjust, but once it had begun all Americans had to stand together simply for self-defense. The Bears had managed to transform an imaginary danger into a real one.

The reality of this danger was made apparent when one messenger returned to report that three of the others sent toward the Marin Peninsula had been captured and two of those killed. A party of twenty Bears mounted up to save the other captured American, and to do battle with hostile Mexicans.

Jose Castro, since Arce had given him the unpleasant news about the horses, had managed to get a large body of cavalry, perhaps sixty or seventy men, across the bay to Marin. They were having breakfast at the ranch of Camilo Ynitia when the Americans stumbled across them.

And "stumbled" is the right word. By the time the Americans reached Olompali what little discipline they had ever had was gone. (There had never been very much; one of the Bears, a particularly irritable individual named "Badger" Smith, had been allowed to go on this expedition only after he insisted he would fight anybody who tried to stop him.) Their horses were tired and strung out. William Ford, nominally their leader, was at the front. All he saw at Olompali was a large corral of horses guarded by a few Mexicans. Without waiting for the rest of his men to catch up he called to the Bears near him to charge. Only in the midst of his charge, when dozens of Mexicans came running from the house, did he realize his mistake.

The Bears, in particular those near Ford, should have been slaughtered. They were outnumbered three to one, and half of these were still straggling along the road. Moreover, they were facing men more skillful as horsemen, and more disciplined as a group. However, the battle of Olompali, as it was called, was determined by what one Bear admitted were "accidental circumstances."

It happened that near the side of the road, on the way to the house, there was a clump of small oaks. There Ford and his group sought cover, and the stragglers (the last of whom was Badger Smith) were just barely able to elude the encircling Mexican horsemen, and to join their fellow Bears among the oaks.

The Mexican leader attempted one charge on the now consolidated American position. The result was one Mexican dead and at least two seriously wounded. The oaks made the superior horsemanship of the Mexicans useless, and provided protection for the American riflemen.

The Americans were surrounded and outnumbered, but to overrun them would cost many lives. A Zeke Merritt would not have hesitated, but Jose de la Torre was a slaughterer of livestock and game, not of men. Later, after they had felt Yankee oppression, the native sons would rise up in the south of California, fight valiantly, and many an American would come to fear the deadly luna. But now was not that time. De la Torre called for retreat, and his men rode off to the south, toward San Rafael.

The battle of Olompali, praised by Ide as having given "tone and character to the Revolution," marked the end of the Bears' republic. John Fremont decided, now that a Mexican town had been occupied and a battle fought, that he could assume leadership of the rebellion in the name of the United States of America. Thus the Bear Flag was replaced by the Stars and Stripes. In a way, this change of flags was inappropriate, for Fremont's men much more than the Bears deserved to fight under the banner of the grizzly. While the Bears had been a rag-tag group whose appearance and pretensions might draw a smile, no one smiled at Fremont's band. One who saw them in 1846 remembered them as "very much sun burnt" and "the most un-uniform, and grotesque set of men I have ever seen." The daughter of a Marin rancher called them simply "demons from hell."

De la Torre was slowed in his retreat south by his wounded. He also seems to have stopped at the ranches along his way to warn of the approaching Americans, and to advise that the ranchers move their families to San Rafael. He stopped at the ranch of James Miller, in particular, to ask him his intentions. As Miller later rememberd the incident, de la Torre was furious at losing a man, so much so that Miller was frightened of a reprisal. He assured the Mexican that he intended to remain entirely neutral, and as a token of his neutrality he offered de la Torre a meal, which was accepted.

The slow pace of de la Torre's retreat almost allowed Fremont and his men to catch him at San Rafael. The most seriously wounded native son had to be left behind. One account has him being hidden in the mission, only to be discovered when Fremont's men noticed fresh blood seeping through the adobe. This particular captive was treated well, and lived to tell the tale. In this he was more fortunate than perhaps he realized at the time.

At about the same time the unburied corpses of the two Bear messengers were found, badly mutilated. Rather than attribute this mutilation to wild animals, the Americans began to believe stories of devilish Mexican torture. The atmosphere was one in which Fremont and his men would thrive.

Shortly after they had set up camp in San Rafael, Carson and another of Fremont's men noticed three Mexicans disembarking at the estuary. One was a young man carrying a message from Castro to de la Torre; another was his twin brother who had decided to accompany him on this adventure; the third was an old man, who was worried about a son in Sonoma. They expected no trouble and were unarmed, but that made no difference.

Kit Carson and the other man shot them dead at a long range, probably without a warning. One version of the event has Carson acting on a direct order from Fremont. Another has him doing it on his own authority. Later some Americans claimed to have found on the dead messenger an order from Castro to murder all American settlers. Other Americans said that the killings were simply a reprisal for the two dead Americans. Another American, who was himself at San Rafael when the killings occured, remembered specifically, "Both men were drunk—an occurence only too common among the warriors at that stage of the campaign." Whether Carson or Fremont was directly responsible for the deaths, the act was in character for both men. Carson would simply have done it as a matter of course, for the fun of it; Fremont would have given it an epic justification.

Fremont's love of the glorious was the undoing of the Americans' attempt to trap de la Torre before he could cross to San Francisco. After leaving San Rafael, the Mexican commander realized how precarious his situation was; to ease it he tried a ruse. He sent an Indian to San Rafael with a message purporting to be from Castro telling of an imminent attack on Sonoma. Fremont's lieutenants, suspicious of intercepting two messengers coming from Castro in so short a time, preferred to finish the business at hand before returning to Sonoma. Fremont, however, ordered a dramatic dash to

relieve the beleaguered fort. When they approached the fort which
had been expecting an attack, they themselves were mistaken for
Castro's troops, and were in danger of being fired upon. While
Carson was calling to the garrison from safe cover, Fremont charged
into the open on his horse so that they might recognize his unmis-
takable figure. Carson seems to have saved the day, but everyone
admired Fremont's heroism.

By the time Fremont had rushed his men back to Marin, de la
Torre was safely off the peninsula, on his way to join Castro. The
situation was somewhat awkward for Fremont. His first campaign
in the California revolution had been left without a single glorious
episode. It would not read well. Fremont decided that he would
cross the bay, and spike the cannons at the San Francisco fort.

The fort, of course, was falling into ruins, and long abandoned.
The cannons had been more than one hundred years old when they
were installed in San Francisco the better part of a century ago. No
one had dared fire them in decades. Moreover, Carson did not like
travelling over water. He is supposed to have said that he would
rather fight a grizzly bear than to cross the bay in one of the available boats. But all that was beside the point. Spiking the Mexican
cannons at San Francisco would be a grandly symbolic gesture.

When he wrote of the episode, Fremont was able to add one
final epic touch. In crossing the strait that separated San Francisco
from Marin he was reminded of the land of Byzantium, that eastern
center of Roman civilization. San Francisco would become the
western center of American civilization, now that it extended, as had
been its destiny, from ocean to ocean, a veritable empire. And as
the Romans had called the strait that led to their great eastern port
the Golden Horn, so Americans now needed a similarly glorious
name for the strait that led to their soon to be great western port.
John Fremont dubbed this treacherous strait, which Kit Carson
feared more than a grizzly, the Golden Gate.

When Jose de la Torre and his men escaped from the Marin
Peninsula, they did so from Sausalito, the ranch of William Richardson; Richardson had suggested to de la Torre that he commandeer
Richardson's boats to make his crossing. When John Fremont decided
to cross the bay to spike the ancient cannons of San Francisco, he
left from Sausalito; and Richardson would joke with the Americans

about the cowardly retreat of the native sons. And when finally the American conquest of southern California was completed, and a treaty with Mexico signed in 1848, the same William Richardson found himself in a most advantageous position, both geographically and personally. He could help to mediate between the native sons and the American conquerors.

This role was not an unaccustomed one for Richardson. British by birth, he had been left at San Francisco in the 1820s by the whaler *Orion* on which he had served as first mate. In 1836, he was awarded the second land grant on the Marin Peninsula, the nineteen thousand southernmost acres. From a fine cove on this land Richardson first showed his dexterity as a middleman between the Mexicans and foreigners, particularly Yankees. Earlier Richardson had served the Californians ferrying supplies around the bay. In 1837 he was made the first captain of the port of San Francisco. Yet the very man whom the Mexican authorities would send to pilot foreign vessels into San Francisco harbor would also show these foreigners how they could avoid the unreasonable Mexican customs. Richardson's cove afforded fresh water and supplies for these ships; it was also reputed to be the center for bay area smuggling. The authorities might make accusations, but Richardson did not flaunt his operations; and he had made himself indispensible.

Richardson was still captain of the port when de la Torre and then Fremont descended upon him in 1846, and he still knew how to please both sides so that each thought it was preferred. And in the first decade of American rule Richardson was again acting as a mediator. While earlier he had shown Yankees how to evade unreasonable Mexican laws, now he showed native sons how to fulfill unreasonable Yankee expectations. These expectations derived from the treaty which the United States had signed with Mexico. This treaty specified that California land grants legitimately issued under Mexican law would be recognized as true titles by the United States. Equitable as this provision might have seemed in the abstract, in practice it could have resulted in great inequity.

The Mexican government itself often did not follow its own rules. (Richardson, for instance, had been granted, besides his Marin ranch, fifty square miles in the northern wilds of California, clearly in excess of the legal maximum permitted by law for a grant.) Moreover, many of the California grantees, for whom custom was so much more important than pieces of writing, had not preserved the documents necessary to establish their claims.

Fortunately, the land commission took a lenient course. Perhaps it had little choice. The commission was badly understaffed, and once an American attorney became familiar with the intricacies of Mexican law he was hired away by one of the prospering firms which represented the land claimants. Despite all this, certain formalities had to be observed. A rancher's claim to have settled and improved a given piece of land had to be verified; signatures on documents had to be confirmed as genuine; and when a document was lacking, someone other than the claimant had to swear that he had seen the document before the rancher had misplaced it.

The star witness before the northern California land commission was William Richardson. In his perfect English he remembered palizidas, adobes, first herds of cattle, lost documents, true signatures. He testified in dozens of different cases. He verified the signatures of more than eighty different persons.

Eventually the native sons began to overreach themselves. Fremont, with his influence, had managed to get the Land Commission to confirm a grant he had brought, to confirm it despite the simple fact that it had never even been seen, let alone improved or occupied, by the alleged grantee. This seemed to invite fraud. Families like the Vallejos made claims for hundreds of thousands of acres. Many claims were made for land grants—two of them on the Marin Peninsula—which had alledgedly been issued only days before the Bear Flag was raised. It was rumored that litigants returned from trips to Mexico with fresh land grants signed by the exiled governor Pio Pico. This particular rumor was confirmed when it was discovered that Pio Pico's signature in the 1850s could in fact be distinguished from his signature in the 1840s, and thereby a number of claims were shown to be fraudulent.

Richardson himself became implicated in this. He took a trip to Mexico where he met a friend in the same town in which Pio Pico's predecessor as governor still lived. As Richardson told the story, he had gone because he heard the rumor that the Americans were going to uphold no coastal land grants. (A ban on coastal land grants was the first of many provisos which were consistently ignored in the actual granting of land.)

Richardson told the story of this trip under cross examination when his friend Jose Limantour applied for recognition of a land grant in 1852. Limantour claimed 16,000 acres, which included both bay islands off the Marin Peninsula and, more importantly, that portion of the San Francisco Peninsula on which a large city was now growing.

Port Captain Richardson had first met Limantour when he had helped the then Captain Limantour salvage much of the cargo of a ship he had run aground at Point Reyes before even reaching San Francisco. (The ship was beached on the sand spit that forms the Coyote's lower lip.) Now he testified for his old friend before the land commission where he was so well known. However, Richardson's testimony was guarded, and even then strongly cross-examined. And well it might have been, for the claim itself was clearly fraudulent. Despite this, somehow the lenient land commission decided favorably. To overturn this decision took more than a year, by which time Limantour had disappeared with the fortune he had made from quickly selling his rights.

While Limantour successfully preyed on the new American order (with a little help from his friends), others attempted to prey on the ranchers. What used to be generosity was soon to become gullibility. And many a rancher learned this only when it was too late. One of these was Timothy Murphy.

There was no reason for Murphy to expect that his prosperity would not continue under the Americans. In fact, he had reason to believe that the old ways might continue on an even larger scale. With the increased population, especially in the gold fields, cattle which used to be worth two or three dollars a head for their hides and tallow were now worth thirty-five dollars for their meat. Suddenly cattle were worth almost as much as sea otter. The California traveler's customary right to kill cattle for food if only he left the hide was definitely a thing of the past.

To test the new order of things, Murphy and a fellow Marin rancher drove a herd of cattle to the gold fields; Murphy returned with probably more money than he had ever made in all his hide and tallow transactions combined. To celebrate, he did what any California rancher would do after particularly good fortune—he threw a huge party that lasted for days, and supposedly cost more than a thousand dollars.

Perhaps it was at this party that Murphy met John Steinburgher, who called himself Baron. Steinburgher not only claimed to be a Baron, he also claimed to represent the War Department of the United States Government. He had come to California to supply the

American military with meat, and had a letter to prove it. Steinburgher chose Timothy Murphy as the first California rancher whom
he was going to make rich quick.

And there was no doubt that the Baron himself was wealthy,
given the style of life he enjoyed in San Francisco. Murphy began
slaughtering large portions of his herds, and shipping the meat over
to the Baron, who could now continue to live like one by quietly
selling it. Murphy did not worry that he was seeing no money; the
United States Government was good for its debts. And the United
States Government did not worry that it was seeing no meat; it was
looking for none. The Baron, however, finally overreached himself;
he was, it seems, spending money more quickly than Murphy could
slaughter cattle. Soon the Baron was bankrupt, and Murphy was
virtually ruined with him.

Murphy still had his land, but there would be no more lavish
parties for him to plan. So he planned for his own death. He had
already sent to Ireland for his heirs, a brother and a nephew. Friends
who now saw him were surprised how quickly he had aged. He was
only in his early fifties but already an old man when he died in 1853.

By 1853 William Richardson was having his own difficulties. In
the early 1850s the turmoil of the Gold Rush had made his Sausalito
harbor a commercial center of the bay region. He had three large
ships operating under his flag, and a number of smaller ones making
shorter runs. He had even tried, unsuccessfully, to have a steam ship
built for him on the East Coast. He had sold land he owned on the
San Francisco Peninsula to buy into the southern California harbor
of San Diego. Richardson was clearly attempting to establish a commercial empire, and San Diego would be his second jewel. As California grew he had only to keep pace with her.

Then the sea, his mastery over which had brought him to
California and had allowed him to prosper there, took back most of
what it had given. In a period of six months all three of his ships were
lost. Perhaps he had expanded so rapidly that he had not selected
sufficiently experienced captains. Whether or not he had chosen his
captains with care, he had failed to insure his cargoes. Even after
he had lost two ships without insurance, he had still trusted his luck.

Now, with all the ships gone, it was a time for judicious retreat.
Richardson needed to sell off portions of his still extensive land holdings to pay his outstanding debts. With the remaining land he and
his family could live a life of modest comfort. Like Murphy, Richard-

son would no longer be able to give lavish parties, and the dream of commercial empire had to be forgotten.

But Richardson would not bend to necessity; he would not seek safe haven. He risked all his land to refinance his shipping line. And at this time, with final land grants still pending, mortgage rates were as high as five percent a month. Quite simply, the rates were too high to give Richardson the time he needed to start again. By 1856 Richardson had lost virtually everything, and his creditors had announced a suit that would take away most of the little that was left. And it was in 1856, at sixty, that, as Richardson's son put it, "the old sea animal crawled ashore to die."

Richardson, Limantour, and Murphy all left their modest marks on the Marin Peninsula. The large cove to the north of Richardson's Sausalito, the cove that Ayala and Santa Maria had named after Our Lady the Mariner, became known as Richardson's Bay. Limantour, safely away with his swindled money, left his name on the sand bar which had initially beached him in California; the Coyote's lower lip is known as Limantour Spit. The bachelor Timothy Murphy did not leave his name on the place; the deposed king of the peninsula, former host of San Rafael Day, left a more touching legacy.

As he had been the largely innocent beneficiary of so much bounty in the Mexican period, so he had been a largely innocent victim in the American period. His generosity had been made gullibility. In his will there was one revealing bequest. As was to be expected, he left all his ranch lands to his brother and nephew—or rather he left all except for six hundred forty acres to the north of San Rafael. There, on the plains where the mission cattle once grazed, Murphy wished the Catholic Church to establish an orphanage. If Murphy had learned anything of history during the past decade, he had learned that it made many orphans.

"It was in the winter of 1835-6 that the ship *Alert,* in the prosecution of her voyage for hides on the remote and almost unknown coast of California, floated into the vast solitude of the Bay of San Francisco. All around was the stillness of nature. One vessel, a Russian, lay at anchor there, but during our whole stay not a sail came or went. . . . Vast banks of fog, invading us from the North Pacific, drove in through the entrance, and covered the whole bay; and when they disappeared we saw a few well-wooded islands, the sandhills on the west, the grassy and wooded slopes on the east, and the vast stretch of the bay to the southward, where we were told lay the Missions of Santa Clara and San Jose, and still lonelier stretches to the northward and north-eastward, where we understood smaller bays spread out, and large rivers, and the few ranchos and missions were remote and widely separated. Not only the neighborhood of our anchorage, but the entire region of the great bay was solitude. On the whole coast of California there was not a lighthouse, a beacon, or a buoy; and the charts were made up from old and disconnected surveys by British, Russian, and Mexican voyagers. Birds of prey and passage swooped and dived about us, wild beasts ranged through the oak groves, and as we slowly floated out of the harbour with the tide, herds of deer came to the water's edge, on the northerly side of the entrance, to gaze at the strange spectacle."

So Richard Dana remembered his first impressions of San Francisco Bay, twenty-four years later. For two years he had served as a crewman on one of the Yankee hide and tallow vessels. He had returned to his native Boston, written a famous account of his two years before the mast, and become a successful New England attorney. Now, in 1859, he returned to survey the progress that Anglo-Saxon America had achieved where once he had been struck by the solitude of nature.

Like many of the Yankees who visited California during the ranch period, Dana had not been impressed with the Mexican native sons and daughters. He regarded them as "an idle and thriftless people." Even the Anglo-Saxons who settled there had not seemed to Dana capable of bringing California out of its solitude. They were, to be sure, possessed of "more industry, frugality, and enterprise than the natives" and "soon get nearly all the trade into their hands." Nonetheless, in order to succeed in California an Anglo-Saxon had to "leave his conscience at Cape Horn." He had to become a Papist, and have his own children raised as Mexicans. In 1835 Dana had doubted that the Anglos of California would be the yeast that would transform the region into a progressive society. "If the 'California fever' (laziness) spares the first generation, it is likely to attack the second."

As Dana's ship collected its hides and tallow, it also needed to take on a supply of wood. For that a launch was sent to Angel Island, called by the pragmatic Yankees "Wood Island." After the wood cutters had been at their work about one week, Dana and four other men were sent to collect the wood which would last them a year. Twenty-four years later he still remembered "Wood Island, where we spent the cold days and nights of December, in our launch." Looking at the island now, Dana understood why the Mexican name had prevailed over the Yankee. The Yankees had been too efficient in their pursuit of wood, and now Angel Island was "clean shorn of trees."

The trees of Wood Island were gone; so was the hide and tallow trade. Dana was struck by this when as he walked among the San Francisco wharves he found a pile of hides lying next to a ship. "What were these hides—what were they not—to us, to me a boy, twenty four years ago? These were our constant labour, our chief object, our almost habitual thought. They brought us out here, they kept us out here, and it was only by getting them that we could escape from the coast and return to home and civilised life." But Dana found that now, in 1859, the trade he knew was already to most Californians "a dim tradition." What hides were still traded were but unimportant parts of larger cargoes.

Nonetheless, Richard Dana, whatever his inclination to nostalgia, did not regret its passing. "The gold discoveries drew off all men from the gathering or cure of hides, the inflowing population made an end of the great droves of cattle." The great droves of cattle had been replaced by great droves of men. Now Anglo-Saxon visitors to San Francisco Bay did not have to yearn for the civilized life of their home. They could find it here in the city—churches, newspapers, hotels. Even approaching San Francisco by ship in the middle of night, one realized that the solitude of nature, the stillness of the sea, no longer controlled the land here.

"Miles out at sea, on the desolate rocks of the Faralones, gleamed the powerful rays of one of the most costly and effective lighthouses in the world. As we drew in through the Golden Gate, another lighthouse met our eyes, and in the clear moonlight of the unbroken California summer we saw, on the right, a large fortification, protecting the narrow entrance.... We bore round the point towards the old anchoring ground of the hide ships, and there, covering the sand-hills and the valleys, stretching from the water's edge to the base of the great hills, and from the old presidio to the mission, flickering all over with the lamps of its streets and houses, lay a city of one hundred thousand inhabitants. Clocks tolled the hour of midnight from its steeples, but the city was alive from the salute of our guns, spreading the news that the fortnightly steamer had come, bringing mails and passengers from the Atlantic world."

Richard Henry Dana approved of all this, as any good New England attorney should have. Only near the end of his visit, when he reached the site of most of his California labor, could Dana no longer bring himself to approve. "The recollections and the emotions all were sad, and only sad.... The past was real. The present, all about me, was unreal, unnatural, repellent." Nothing was left of any of the old hide houses. Dana took faint pleasure in the few broken bricks at what he thought was the site of one. The only enduring thing he could find at the place was a sound in the night air, the coyote's bark. And he found what consolation he could in it. "The coyotes still bark in the woods, for they belong to no man, and are not touched by his changes."

VII
Marin County

On August 2, 1872, John Dwinelle stood before an assembled crowd in San Rafael to deliver the featured oration at the ceremonial laying of the cornerstone for the new Marin Courthouse. Less than a year before he had delivered an oration at the dedication of the San Francisco City Hall. On that earlier occasion, he had, skillfully, chosen the right things to say. He had talked generally of the "instinct of civilization that every enlightened people should select some favored spot, and stamp it as the center of its power, by the erection of monuments which symbolize at once its advancement, its institutions, its tastes, and its hopes for the future." But he also spoke specifically of the achievement of San Francisco, the very progress that had so impressed Richard Henry Dana. "We were in the midst of chaos, but we knew that the whirling forces were the elements of empire." The new Californians were taming these forces to their own advantage, and this building would stand as a symbol of their enduring achievement. So confident were they, their spokesman could even view the ceaseless shiftings of nature with equanimity: "The ever-moving sea presents an emblem of the unrest, the ceaseless activity, and ultimate success of our commercial empire."

This speech had been so successful that Dwinelle now found himself with a new audience in San Rafael. This was to be the first true courthouse for Marin County. Until now county business had to be conducted in the old adobe ranch house of Timothy Murphy, a situation all progressive citizens regarded as a disgrace to the new society they were building.

The new courthouse, unlike the ruins which passed for a courthouse at present, was to be built mostly of wood, a more precise and enduring substance than the primitive adobe. It was to have a Greek temple facade, dominated by large Corinthian columns. Within, the offices, court, and jail were to be laid out on a cruciform floorplan, which included a high-domed entry hall suitable for public hangings.

Such were the plans that John Dwinelle had come to San Rafael to praise. He could not perhaps praise these plans as effusively as he had praised the San Francisco City Hall months before. This courthouse was not to be the symbolic center for an empire, commercial or otherwise. This was a provincial town, a small, relatively unimportant part of the growing empire. Nonetheless, Dwinelle could dignify the occasion by praising the impulse to build generally.

"Man, the moment that he emerges from the savage state, becomes a builder. His constructions mark his progress; their ruins indicate the degree of his civilization." As Dwinelle expanded eloquently upon this generalization, as he spoke of cavemen, the Aztecs, ancient Rome, Versailles, he could perhaps see some eyes in his audience looking past him, to where the mission once had been.

The site of the new courthouse was only a few yards away from where the Franciscans had established their mission. Nothing of the mission building stood any longer; just a decade before a carpenter had paid the county for the right to raze the remaining structures for any beams that might be salvaged from the adobe. (Elsewhere in town what was said to be an orchard wall was still standing; it would last until the Masons decided to build a hall there.) The mission was not easily incorporated into Dwinelle's oration.

He did speak of the missionaries, "the simple-minded men [who] came here and erected the first buildings constructed in Marin County." But this was a disturbing subject. Dwinelle had to speak of what had become of their work. "Their buildings have toppled into heaps. The very bones of the missionaries and of other converts have become absorbed into the soil." Was this, according to Dwinelle, to be the ultimate result of man's impulse to build?

Such a question could not be heard in a center such as San Francisco, amidst the noise and excitement of an empire being built. But here, in this less important and quieter place, with a new cornerstone being laid within sight of earlier ruins, it was harder to avoid. How was Dwinelle to assure his listeners, these builders of a new temple of justice—how was he to assure them that their impulse to build a new society would be better treated by time, that the ruins of their building would not be razed for salvage?

He could demean the missionaries as simple-minded men, and also assure his listeners that "the spot consecrated fifty years ago to benevolence and religion will always be holy ground." He could appeal to his own audience's sense of superiority; they, after all, were "responding to the next higher instinct of civilization." But was there within the historical whirl a benediction for human virtue, a secure foundation for a just temple?

What Dwinelle had come to say had been profoundly disrupted by the emptiness his listeners could see over his shoulder. The mission had disappeared before the courthouse had come into existence: ashes to ashes, dust to dust, the beginning and the end were before their eyes in a single moment. To break this spell, and to give a fitting conclusion, Dwinelle appealed to what he could see beyond his listeners, the permanence of the mountain.

"Behold lofty Tamalpais as he rears his sublime purple form into the sky! He looks down upon us, not with forty centuries but perhaps with forty thousand centuries as

'He rears his awful form

High from the vale, and midday leaves the storm.'

What has he not seen?"

As Dwinelle's peroration continued, he recounted what this impersonal witness had seen. He had seen California as "a submerged lake, her mountains only islands." He had heard seeds drop, and heard too the redwoods they became. He had seen the Indians inherit the land, and had watched the Europeans coast in his shadow. He had seen the Spanish come, and had seen them supplanted by a modern civilization. He had seen all the flux that had here been. "And now he looks down upon us, as we look upon the sea, and dedicate this site to Law and Justice, and write upon its granite tablets the solemn approval of the people."

The consolation John Dwinelle could offer was the unconscious witness of an impersonal peak. The Marin *Journal* reported, "The oration was listened to with earnest attention, and all seemed to realize the importance of the occasion." The courthouse itself was completed in seven months, and had stood for almost a century, when it was burned to the ground in a spectacular fire.

The man who should have given the cornerstone oration in 1872 was not John Dwinelle, but Oscar Lovell Shafter. This was not because Shafter was a more experienced orator than Dwinelle. Nor was it primarily because Shafter, unlike Dwinelle, was a prominent landowner in Marin, although Shafter was perhaps the wealthiest man in Marin at a time when wealth and social standing were almost equivalent. The reasons Shafter deserved to address the crowd in San Rafael that day lay far deeper.

The Marin Peninsula in the 1850s and 1860s had been a turbulent place; it was as if the new American society was bent upon killing itself before it had truly been born. And to many, the laying of the cornerstone for a courthouse must have been a sign that the worst of these times was over.

Oscar Shafter should have been the speaker at the dedication because his life in California, more than Dwinelle's, and perhaps as much as any other prominent American in Marin, had touched the whole of that struggle. And he had lived through these twenty years in California with the hope that a day like this one would come, a day when the destructive, at times almost demonic, forces at work within the new society would somehow transcend themselves and make all that went before seem little more than a fortunate fall. Oscar Shafter thought about events in such exalted terms, even in the worst of times.

The worst of times on the Marin Peninsula had perhaps been the 1850s. The uncertainty of the land titles at that time had encouraged land speculation; men would buy the right to large tracts of land, as much as possible on credit, and then try to elude their creditors until some bonanza or other was realized. One speculator, for instance, had for a time controlled both the Reed and Cooper ranches where he was going to found a city that would eventually dwarf San Francisco—or so he thought.

Another speculator, Dr. Andrew Randall, benefitting from his prominence as both a former state legislator and president of the nascent California Academy of Science, bought the whole of the Point Reyes Peninsula almost entirely on credit. Randall had not one or two but many creditors who were, with increasing unwillingness, financing his $250,000 gamble. And Randall was particularly adroit at avoiding them. Attempts to foreclose were complicated by both Randall's own legal maneuvering and the corruption of the Marin County sheriff who (it seemed) would serve anything on anybody for a price. Finally, one creditor traced Randall to a San Francisco hotel, and in the lobby shot him through the head, only to be lynched himself two days later before an appreciative crowd.

Oscar Shafter had been representing one of Randall's creditors when the doctor was murdered. Shafter was a New England attorney who had been called to San Francisco to participate in the lucrative land title litigation. Now he saw an opportunity to gain land for himself. Only a skillfull attorney, knowledgeable in the California land titles, could hope to free Point Reyes from the complex legal tangle in which Randall had left it. To anyone else the land would be only trouble. But such an attorney—with some shrewd maneuvering—could have in his hands fifty thousands acres at a fraction of their true value.

Shafter bought out his client's interest, and gradually gained the whole of Point Reyes for his family. (His brother had recently joined his law firm.) For title to the main portion of the peninsula, a portion which on paper had cost Randall $150,000, Shafter paid $15,000 at a public auction.

That Shafter should have been brought to prominence on Marin as the result of a murder was itself appropriate, for violence was even more characteristic of this new society than legal tangles and land speculation. Most of the western half of the Marin Peninsula had become a series of lumber boom towns which were mining the redwood forests to build Gold Rush San Francisco (and rebuild it when parts of it repeatedly burned down). The western Marin forests were producing a million board feet of lumber a year, with lumber selling at two dollars a board foot in San Francisco. But violence had become so commonplace in these boom towns that a reporter ended his story of one particularly senseless killing with the sentence: "This is the seventh, eighth, or ninth man that has been murdered on Tomales Bay during the last few years, the author of the deed in each instance escaping punishment." Seventh, eighth, or was it the ninth? Unsolved murders were occuring at such a rate among the few hundred people in the lumbering area that the reporter was having a difficult time keeping count.

The Mexican families who had settled there, and were now drifting toward poverty, were not spared the violence. One grantee was said to have been poisoned to death by a disgruntled servant. The sixty year old widow of Rafael Garcia was shot to death by a rejected suitor, who then turned the gun on himself. One of the murders of 1861 was committed because a rancher had allowed his stock to graze on his neighbor's land; and this murderer, although convicted, was never punished.

The weakness of law-enforcement led to vigilantism, but there were always members of the society like Shafter who were convinced that this apparent chaos was really an emerging order misunderstood. Shafter himself had a personal triumph on Point Reyes, one that laid the foundation for a family fortune. Yet it was more than that, for Shafter believed he had achieved on Point Reyes what had to be achieved on the Marin Peninsula—indeed, in the state as a whole. He had found a way, through his prudence, skill, and ambition, to use the violence, speculation, and corruption of others to his own advantage, and thereby to achieve a new legally recognized order on Point Reyes from which many could benefit.

The broader social significance of what Shafter had accomplished is perhaps best suggested by a single fact. When the last appeal on the last case that would give the Shafter family clear title to Point Reyes reached the California Supreme Court, one Justice had to disqualify himself as an interested party—Oscar Lovell Shafter. The legal order he had established on Point Reyes for his family he was now helping establish on the whole state.

Thus, Shafter in 1872 was not only the head of the wealthiest landowning family in Marin, he was also one of the most distinguished members of the bar. He was a jurist whom John Dwinelle would eventually praise for his large mind adept at applying the reason of the law to the variety of human circumstance. This eminence within the legal profession would have made Shafter a particularly appropriate choice for the cornerstone oration. Yet there was an even deeper reason, a reason few at the time would have fully understood.

In a society in which there were so many transients, so much instability, such violence, a society in which government had yet to become an effective agent for public order, respectable citizens felt the need to organize into voluntary associations which would promote stability, morality, and progress. This need could not be met by the churches, since by their creeds they tended to divide this religiously pluralistic society. Rather, this need was met by the growth of semi-secret fraternal orders: the Oddfellows, the Druids, the Knights of the Red Branch, and, most prominently, the Masons.

At the simplest level the fraternity offered itself as a buffer between the individual brother and the society as a whole. The fraternity operated as an insurance company. A brother ill or out of work would be given a weekly allowance, the size depending upon his standing within the fraternal hierarchy. And, of course, the brothers would be expected individually to do what they could to assist the advancement of their fellows within society. The fraternity also provided death benefits for a family bereaved of a brother, again the amount depending upon the brother's standing.

A Mason, a Druid or an Oddfellow was expected to believe in a Divine Principle, a belief which assured that good was somehow rewarded, evil somehow punished; the evil destroy themselves, while the good build a better future for all. The Masons and others had elaborate rituals which gave the brothers esoteric symbols to strengthen their sense of themselves as a moral elite. (Oddfellows thought themselves not odd, but unusual.) And this sense of worth would help them in their work to protect each other, and to improve society generally.

So strong had the Masons become on the Marin Peninsula by 1872 (and so weak the older Catholic families) that the courthouse ceremony was given over to them. The cornerstone was laid according to masonic ritual, including the singing of "Hail Masonry Divine." The Masons must have been pleased with John Dwinelle as an orator. Dwinelle, himself at this time both a Freemason and an Oddfellow, had developed the traditional masonic theme of the great builders of history. Best of all, he had ended his oration with the phrase "So mote it be!" which only the Masons would have recognized as their peculiar form of Amen.

Oscar Shafter was no Mason, nor did he belong to any other fraternal organization. This perhaps in itself would have disqualified him as a speaker. Yet Shafter, more than Dwinelle or probably anyone else who was at San Rafael that day, had thought seriously and sympathetically about the historical significance of the masonic and other secular fraternities. He himself had been deeply touched by the Unitarianism of his native New England, and he approved entirely of its rejection of the supernatural facade of Christianity for the sake of its humanistic core.

A few years before Dwinelle's oration, Shafter had given a lengthy address in which he had tried to make clear the two elements in Medieval Christianity that had most impeded modern progress. The first was a dogmatic respect for past tradition; one must believe that something new and better can be born in the present. The second was a belief in the demonic; one must respect the intellect as wholly good, see ignorance as the source of all human evil, and therefore reject as a contradiction the very idea of an evil intelligence.

Such a philosophy, with its attendant fear of Roman Catholicism as the embodiment of reaction, Shafter shared with the Masons and the Oddfellows. But Shafter, because of his Unitarian roots, saw with particular clarity the affirmations required to sustain such a philosophy. Dwinelle, confronted with the remains of Mission San Rafael, appealed to Mount Tamalpais to give a sense of higher meaning to the present enterprise. Shafter would not have relied on vague personification.

Throughout his life he had been preoccupied with memory. For him there were personal painful memories. He had lost his mother when still a boy. While he was first in California seeking his fortune, five of his seven children died in Vermont in a diphtheria epidemic. Shafter cherished his memories, the only living thing that was left for him of these loved ones. His favorite gift to a young person was always a diary.

One of Shafter's daughters learned well from him. As an old woman, she published a biography of her father to which she placed as the epigraph a quotation from one of his favorite histories: "All things hasten to decay; all fall, all perish. Man dieth, iron consumeth, wood decayeth, towns crumble, strong walls fall down, the rose withereth away; the war horse waxeth feeble, gay trappings grow old; all the works of man's hands perish. Thus are we taught that all die, both clerk and lay; and short would be the fame of any after death if their history did not endure, by being written in the book of the clerk."

However, for Shafter, even such an affirmation of the endurance of the public memory as recorded by "the clerk" would not have been enough to give meaning to human experience. That a historian or an admiring daughter should happen to record parts of a life was good. But Shafter sought his consolation, and the consolation of the human race, not in the occasional records of the historian but in the enduring memory of the universal human soul, the transcending spirit of human history which, using individuals as its instruments, progresses, and never perishes, and never acts vainly, and never forgets. About this Shafter was certain, as he wrote in his own diary.

"Memorials graven upon sculptured marble may be worn away by an imperceptible abrasion, the records of desolation written upon the earth's surface by the volcano and the earthquake, the fierce chronicles of human guilt and of Almighty Justice, effaced by other changes, may bear no witness to succeeding generations of the retribution they were designed to commemorate. But the soul unerringly retains all, even its faintest impressions, in all places, under all circumstances in all times. Immortal in itself, in its most transient reflections, its slightest emotions, its briefest and least important speculations, all, all of them indelibly retained."

Oscar Lovell Shafter should have been on the podium in 1872 to heroically affirm the cumulative meaning of human experience, to affirm that the spirit of the mission still persisited in the courthouse, the mass in the masonic ritual—to affirm that all the human soul had enjoyed, observed, or endured on this peninsula was somehow still here to give wholeness to the present, and to assure the future. But Oscar Shafter could not even be invited to the courthouse ceremony, although he still lived on Point Reyes. The universal human spirit had discarded Oscar Shafter without killing him. Only in his sixties, he had become prematurely senile. His brother described him now as an "unhappy paradox...outliving the death of all that was himself." And Shafter's legal reputation was described by a friend as a "splendid column" which now stood "amidst the majestic ruins of the intellect which built it."

When John Dwinelle invoked Mount Tamalpais in his peroration, without knowing it he was invoking that feature of nature which was now the chief impediment to progress in Marin County. The grizzly bear was long extinct on the peninsula. The coyote might still bark in the woods, but poison and traps doomed him as well. It was geography itself which most obviously defied human will.

The ridge of which Mount Tamalpais was the highest part effectively divided the Marin Peninsula into two separate sections. There were few wagon roads directly across it, except at the very north of the peninsula where the ridges descended into the plains once frequented by antelope. This left San Rafael, the county seat, remote from the prospering lumber towns on the far side of the ridge.

Moreover, geographical division deepened contrary political loyalties, especially in the troubled times of the Civil War. The unruly coastal region was loyal to the north, and ardently supported Lincoln. Bolinas, the chief lumber port, voted for Lincoln 91 to 24, and another coastal precinct favored him 77 to 1. In contrast, many southerners had settled the bayside; a school district had actually been incorporated under the name "Dixie." The Marin *Journal*, the

only newspaper of the county, had been founded in San Rafael to
provide reliable news of the Civil War, and thereby to counteract
"Secesh" rumors. Despite its efforts, the bayside of Marin was
clearly, if not secessionist, at least opposed to the uncompromising
policy of Lincoln. San Rafael voted against him 80 to 36, and in
one bayside precinct Lincoln lost 22 to 2. The editor of the Marin
Journal perhaps consoled himself that his effort on behalf of Lincoln
might have provided the small margin by which he carried the
county. The editor did remain strictly neutral in the various efforts
to have the county seat removed from San Rafael, efforts which
failed apparently only because the opponents could not agree among
themselves on a new seat.

As the ridge divided the county into two distinct communities,
so the various ribs which this spine of the peninsula sent toward the
bay thwarted development of the bayside itself. These lesser ridges
made transportation of goods by land expensive, much more expensive than transportation by water. And the legal boundaries of Marin
County made this worse.

Marin was not one of the original counties proposed to the state
legislature; in the original report it was to be a part of Sonoma,
much as it had been in Vallejo's time. Marin was only added as a
county when the legislature decided the report had been too conser-
vative. The newly formed County of Marin had its boundaries set at
the pleasure of its two powerful neighbors, San Francisco and
Sonoma.

San Francisco was given boundaries that extended to Marin's
low water mark; Angel Island, and even ships at anchor in Richardson's Bay, would be under the legal jurisdiction of San Francisco.
Although the two natural landmarks for Marin's northern boundary
would appear to be a natural oceanside port to the north of Point
Reyes, and the Petaluma, a navigable river which drains Marin's
northern plains and empties into the bay, the boundaries were
legally drawn so that both of these were effectively within the control of Sonoma. As a result, goods being transported from San
Francisco to counties north of Marin would by-pass it entirely; in
particular, they would be carried by boat up the Petaluma River.

By 1870 the river-port town of Petaluma had become the sixth
largest city in the state. Moreover, it was the natural commercial
center for Marin, San Rafael existing only in its shadow. For instance, the ferry connection of San Rafael to San Francisco existed

only because San Rafael was a secondary stop on the important Petaluma run. Moreover, the ferry would not pull in close to San Rafael, but rather stopped at the end of a bay peninsula a few miles away, miles across marshland over which the San Rafael leaders could not seem to keep a decent road. As geography had made Petaluma prosper, so it had also apparently destined San Rafael and the rest of the Marin Peninsula (even western Marin once the lumber played out) to remain undeveloped, while everywhere else in the bay region progress seemed unstoppable.

In the 1860s there had been an attempt to bring Petaluma into Marin County. This was successfully opposed by both Marin and Sonoma leaders. Sonoma did not want to lose a prosperous town, and the residents of Marin did not want their votes swamped by the more numerous Petalumans. The attempt to graft progress onto the Marin Peninsula failed. And so Marin seemed destined to languish. Unless, that is, Americans could somehow gain dominance over the hostile terrain as once the horseman had come to dominate the grizzly. Then Marin would provide the depots for goods going to and from the north; and Petaluma would languish.

By the time the cornerstone for the new courthouse was laid, the means for so dominating the terrain was at hand; in effect replacing the skeleton of the peninsula with one created for human convenience. There was now on the peninsula a new horse, one made of iron.

"What a contrast is felt between 'now' and 'then.' *Then*, comers and goers to and from San Rafael had to pack into coaches and lumbering mud wagons, pile up on top and hang to the sides, stow away in the boot, and then linger from one-half to three-quarters of an hour between town and steamboat landing.... Now we trip down to the depot, a short distance from the hotels, wait on the platforms a few minutes for the last tap of the bell, step into an elegant car, and in eight or ten minutes step off of the car into the steamer."

Thus did a newspaper writer describe the difference made by the modest railroad that had been run across the marsh in 1870, from San Rafael to the ferry terminal. Little more than a streetcar line in itself, it portended a successful end to the struggle of Marin County against Mount Tamalpais. This short stretch of track, as much as anything, justified the laying of a permanent foundation for a new courthouse.

Actually there had been railroad fever on the Marin Peninsula since the late 1860s when work on the transcontinental railroad was drawing to a close. In 1869 a San Francisco and Sausalito Railroad was projected which would have its southern terminus at William Richardson's old rancho, Sausalito. One financier dismissed the whole idea of a railroad connecting land only "fit for coyotes." And the Marin *Journal* was sceptical: "New Sausalito is emphatically a big thing—on paper."

The doubts were in fact justified. The men who were behind the new railroad had, before announcing it, bought large tracts of land along the proposed route, land the value of which multiplied once the announcement was made. Then the owners of the imaginary railroad, having begun construction, sold their land for a handsome profit, and stopped construction.

However, the very next year the North Pacific Coast Railroad Company of California was incorporated. The leaders of this corporation owned large tracts of virgin forest on the north coast of California. A railroad would make lumbering this timber profitable. Even more plausibility was given this enterprise by the deep involvement of the Shafter family of Point Reyes.

In 1872 Marin County voters approved a subsidy of $160,000 for the railroad. Towns that were to be left off the proposed route voted against it; for example, Bolinas, for which the railroad meant the end of even the remant of its prosperity as a lumber port, voted twenty to one against the subsidy. But the route was carefully planned to move from a Sausalito terminus through most of the population centers, notably San Rafael and Tomales; and the subsidy passed overwhelmingly. A new age seemed to be dawning.

Trouble, however, began almost immediately. Apparently the route had been drawn with too much regard for voting towns and too little for terrain. As an editor of the Marin *Journal* explained it, the population of Tomales and the proffered wealth of the Shafters and others who lived nearby forced the railroad executives to route it through "a dead country without any traffic possibilities except the shipment of a few boxes of butter, instead of building through a a country of vast resources." Of course, the people of Tomales did not regard theirs as the dead country of the peninsula.

Directors of the new railroad, for their part, said simply that engineering surveys now showed that the subsidy was too small. To cut directly from San Rafael to Tomales meant to cross the ridge at White's Hill, a more expensive feat of engineering than first thought.

The directors had two alternatives for the three-man county board of supervisors. The first, which must have been only a ploy, suggested a new route, one that would benefit Sonoma as much as Marin. (Woe to the supervisor who used Marin money to help Petaluma to lengthen its shadow over the peninsula!) The second alternative was to double the subsidy.

The supervisors, however, held firm; the subsidy the voters approved specified a route across White's Hill; if the railroad wanted its $160,000, it would have to follow this route; and it would get no more than that.

The railroad representatives then presented a third alternative, which perhaps had been in their minds all along. If they could not skirt the spine of the peninsula, perhaps they could skirt one of its ribs. To bring the rails directly from Sausalito to San Rafael required transversing a particularly awkward ridge just to the south of the county seat. Yet the valley in which this beautiful town of San Rafael was nestled formed a T with another valley running north-south, a valley which virtually pointed to Sausalito. The railroad could save an estimated forty thousand dollars if it was allowed to run its tracks along this valley. At the junction of the two valleys the main line would turn west toward White's Hill, and a spur could be run back the two miles to San Rafael.

This proposal, a small compromise to save an important project, seemed eminently reasonable to most progressive-minded Marin leaders, except those who happened to reside or hold land in San Rafael. The county seat on a spur? The civic leaders of San Rafael demanded that the supervisors act responsibly, and reject this violation of the original agreement. The supervisor from San Rafael heartily concurred, but the other two supervisors thought that a slight inconvenience to San Rafael was a small price to pay for progress. By a vote of two to one the new route was approved; and in Bolinas there must have been a few wan smiles.

However, San Rafael, unlike Bolinas, was not without resources. Its leading citizen, William Tell Coleman, had been the greatest leader of the San Francisco vigilantes. Now San Rafael, the town of his summer mansion, was his pet project. He had organized a water company and various other civic improvements. Under his feisty leadership, San Rafael harrassed the new railroad company with suits which for a time successfully held up payment of the subsidy. Eventually the road beds were laid and the four tunnels bored through the rock. When the tunnel at White's Hill was finally finished, there was a celebration, complete with toasts of chilled champagne. The spine of the peninsula had been broken.

When the tracks reached what was now called simply the Junction, the railroad president, in a gesture of friendship, set a date for the completion of the spur to San Rafael. His men would work day and night so that the first North Pacific Coast train would reach San Rafael by July 25, 1874. But the simple stunt of having men work all night did not impress Coleman. Even when this promise was made good, William Coleman was not impressed. Coleman liked a good fight, and the North Pacific Coast Railroad was going to know it had been in one. Coleman's town, for which he had donated parks and introduced gas lighting, was not going to be at the end of a spur. San Rafael continued its suit, and looked for ways to cause more trouble. Coleman and San Rafael found an unlikely ally in this cause in their old rival Petaluma.

In Petaluma, as in most California towns of this period, there had been much railroad agitation. But railroad development was not in the interest of a river port such as Petaluma. This was stated clearly in the Petaluma *Argus* when a railroad was first proposed with Petaluma as its southern terminus. "Are we sure Petaluma will remain the terminus of the road?" The railroad, the writer maintained, would be a danger rather than an aid to Petaluma's prosperity, "a tornado, threatening to reduce us from a flourishing inland city as the head of navigation to a mere railroad station!"

Of course, there was something worse than being a mere railway station; that was not being one in a land where the railroad was the dominant mode of transportation. And by the 1870s California was being transformed into such a land. Towns like Petaluma were forced to salvage what they could of their old prosperity.

The leaders of Petaluma realized this only when a town in the Napa Valley to the east began to project a railroad of their own into northern country that Petalumans had come to regard as their commercial province. As one leader put it bluntly, "Unless speedy action be taken there is great danger that a road from Napa will swing around us into the Russian River Valley taking from us all the up-country trade and travel." Now a Petaluma railroad became a sacred obligation, for not to build one would be "to acknowledge ourselves behind the progressive spirit of civilization at least half a century."

Perhaps such high sounding phrases led the leaders to overestimate their present position. They did get their railroad. And it was led by perhaps the ablest of the local railroad presidents who were the true successors to the Vallejos of the Mexican period, Peter Donahue.

Donahue had worked in Glasgow factories as a child; as a teenager he had apprenticed to a machinist in New Jersey; from there he had sought his fortune first in Peru and then in Gold Rush San Francisco. He soon realized that his skill as a machinist could be the making of his fortune in California while others were gambling on gold. His first foundry was established in a tent; but by the 1860s his tent days were past. He was the owner of the prosperous Union Iron Works. These works in turn gave him a competitive edge in the bidding on local railroads; he could supply himself with his own machines.

First Donahue had established a short, commuter railroad that connected San Francisco to its southern suburbs. Once this railroad proved profitable, he immediately sold out to a larger line. Then Donahue turned his eyes to the north. In 1868 he was president of what he called the San Francisco and North Pacific Railroad. He had decided to be the railroad baron of the north bay region, and he was willing to do whatever was required.

Peter Donahue was not a man to trifle with, particularly as the Petalumans tried to do once the railroad reached their town. They decided they did not want the tracks where Donahue wanted them. They refused him the right of way, except where they wished it. In response, Donahue simply gave the Petaluma leaders a lesson on who controlled the forces of progress. He built the tracks where they wanted, but continued them straight past the town down the river, a few miles closer to the bay. The terminus of his railroad would no longer be in ungrateful Petaluma, but at a new town which he graciously named Donahue.

So, like San Rafael, Petaluma had a grudge against its railroad. And the two towns were united by their common desire to be a terminus, or at least a major station, on a railroad. They had both been, at least temporarily, and certainly unwillingly, left behind by the great spirit of progress, which these days seemed somehow dependent upon the caprice of railroad executives.

In October, 1874, in Novato (a village halfway between), the leaders of Petaluma and San Rafael met to plan to build their own railroad which would have both Petaluma and San Rafael as termini. However, even as work on this railroad began, as land was leveled and tracks laid, it must have been apparent to all concerned that the alliance of San Rafael and Petaluma could only be temporary.

The new line would never have enough business to be economically feasible unless it was absorbed by a larger, already existing line. And only two railroads could be interested, the North Pacific Coast or Donahue's. If North Pacific Coast took over, then Petaluma would be the terminus for its line from the Junction, a line now too long to be called just a spur. If Donahue took over, then San Rafael would be the terminus for a railroad that would then rival the North Pacific Coast.

In the end, there was little competition for this line, due partly to Coleman's continuous harrassment of the North Pacific Coast Railroad. In order to soothe San Rafael, North Pacific Coast had just absorbed, at considerable expense, San Rafael's ferry connection. Moreover, the North Pacific Coast was just reaching the timber that was supposed to provide its margin of profit, and hence was in no financial condition for further expansion. So the railroad went to Donahue.

A San Rafael newspaper could print that "our thriving town" had been freed from being "the abused slave to a tyrant monopoly." The leaders of Petaluma could only accuse themselves of having helped forge another link in the tyrant Donahue's chain. And they could glumly look forward to the day when Donahue, having pushed his road past San Rafael to a ferry terminal he had built to the south, would cease ferry service altogether to the Petaluma river.

On the day that Peter Donahue was supposed to open his San Rafael station, despite the fact that it was not quite finished, there was held a celebration. The speeches at this celebration are not hard to imagine, at least for anyone who has read Shafter, Dwinelle or their like. One can imagine the historical accounts of man's triumph over nature, the evocations of the spirit of civilization and its onward rush, of the iron horse as the present instrument of progress, and of Peter Donahue as the maker of history. Donahue himself saw things in plainer terms, as he made clear in his own brief speech.

"I feel deeply the complimentary things you have said in reference to myself and the enterprise we are now inaugurating, and I scarcely know how to thank you and the people of your town and county who are now present. But I desire to say that I entered upon this enterprise in a business point of view. I thought, and I think now, that there is something in it for me, and I am fully convinced that the best way to make it remunerative to me is to do that which will be pleasing and satisfactory to you. And so I propose to carry you safely, speedily, and pleasantly to and from your handsome little town, and I propose to do it cheaply. I want you all to ride with me, but I want you to pay your fare. As business increases, as I think it will, I will reduce rates, because while I wish to live myself, I am willing that you shall live also.

"We had intended to have a little collation here today, but our depot is not completed, and in this we are disappointed, but if you will get aboard of the cars we will take you to Petaluma and bring you back. We have sandwiches and wine enough for the ladies and whiskey enough for the men. Get aboard—quick!"

Peter Donahue died in 1885, in his sixties, his railroad thriving. He had been inspecting his Marin terminal, caught a chill, and a little more than a week later was dead. A eulogistic biography that appeared at the time explained, "His original rugged constitution had been impaired by overwork in the eager pursuit of business."

Donahue in his bluff way would have had little patience with any attempt to sentimentalize his death, for he had had little patience with the attempts to sentimentalize any other aspect of his life. A number of years before his death his workmen had presented him with a gold-headed rosewood walking stick. The reason the men gave him the cane was made clear by what they had engraved on it.

Donahue had refused to hire Chinese workers. The work-crews who built the railroads, and built most everything else in late nineteenth century California, were predominantly either Irish or Chinese. The Shafter-supported railroad had been built almost entirely by Oriental labor; the Freemasons and Lincoln-supporters as a group preferred to supervise oriental laborers. But Donahue stood fast, and hired only caucasians. And when his men praised him for this and presented him with the rosewood cane, he accepted the cane, but added, "Everything I ever got in this country I got out of the bone and sinews of whitemen."

Donahue had gotten a great deal out of the whitemen; he had lived like a baron. It was only fitting that the getting and keeping of it should have taken a little out of his own bones and sinews. He should have died, as he did, from the eager pursuit of business.

The ruin of William Coleman was of a more spectacular type. "The lion of the vigilantes," as he was called, was a victim of his own ambition. Through most of the 1880s he continued to lead San Rafael in its improvement. The town, now incorporated, had a water system, fire department, a new park, a new schoolhouse. The leaders of San Rafael could not have been surprised to find their own William Coleman being praised on a heroic scale in a San Francisco newspaper of 1887.

"When such men as William T. Coleman lend their energies to the accomplishment of any desired end, the chances—or rather the results, for chance then ceases to be an element in the matter—are that success is attained. It could hardly be otherwise with a man who refuses to see anything but the final object which he has in view, and paying no heed to the obstacles which intervene except to over-come them, presses directly on his course until the final end has been successfully attained."

But what must have surprised even Coleman's most ardent ad-mirers in San Rafael was how far Coleman was reaching. He was al-lowing himself to be promoted as a western challenger to Grover Cleveland's renomination for the presidency by the Democratic Party. A leader of San Rafael as a candidate for president! This was far more significant than Shafter's tenure as State Supreme Court Justice, or even the coming selection of a San Rafael Freemason as Grand Master for the whole state.

There was strong opposition to Cleveland's renomination, particularly because of his support of lowered tariffs. Praise of Coleman had found its way into a New York newspaper: "good mixer, a brilliant speaker, a most lucid thinker, and, above all, a remark-ably well-balanced businessman who would certainly swing the West and might even carry N.Y. State." In California even a Republican newspaper wrote: "No man in California stands higher than he in point of integrity, brains, and courage."

Coleman opposed Cleveland on the tariff issue because at this very time he had extended his own financial resources to the limit in order to develop borax mining in the California desert, borax being a commodity protected by tariff. Once these mines began to produce fully, Coleman would become an immensely wealthy man, of such wealth that he could begin to think on a national scale. In 1887, however, the mines had yet to produce sufficiently to justify his expenditure. And then after Cleveland's renomination a law was passed which, in keeping with his general policy against tariffs, removed borax itself from the list. The simple signing of this act into law ruined Coleman financially. He became the prey of his creditors.

So Coleman's considerable energies were now completely absorbed in simply staving off bankruptcy. Gradually all of his holdings were sold off at a fraction of their worth. (Latter day Shafters would try to lay the basis of their fortunes on his demise.) This included both his San Francisco and his San Rafael mansions. After four years of struggle and maneuvering he had finally avoided bankruptcy, and a year later, 1893, he was dead. This same year, there was published in Coleman's town of San Rafael a *Souvenir* which portrayed the new Marin County which Coleman and those like him had striven to bring into reality.

"Hitherto, thousands have been deterred from purchasing land and building homes here, because they were unwilling to live in a section so lacking in transportation facilities. This objection removed, they are desirous of availing themselves of the privileges of residence which this county so abundantly presents. It is confidently believed that the residence portion of Marin County will more than double in population in the next five years. The county has never yet been 'boomed', and its advantages have never been properly advertised; yet its population has suddenly increased, and is now increasing more rapidly than for some time past. New homes are being built in every town. The valleys are being dotted with country seats and summer homes.... New and more boats and trains will transport a much larger number of 'San Francisco Marin residents' next year than this, and every subsequent year the rate of increase will be larger."

The authors could present persuasive evidence that the bayside of Marin was about to be "boomed." What was going to happen in sites throughout the county was already happening at the base of Mount Tamalpais. Almost overnight a new town, Mill Valley, had been created there.

As late as 1887 there had been only one small group of buildings in the vicinity, the Blithedale Hotel and its cottages, originally established in 1878 as a sanitarium, now also caring for vacationers weary of urban life. This hotel was reasonably successful, as were many similar enterprises on the bayside of Marin. Mount Tamalpais and its ridge protects Mill Valley and many of the other areas of the eastern Marin Peninsula from the fogs which sweep through the mountainless San Francisco Peninsula even in the summer. So shivering San Franciscans could look across the Golden Gate to protected valleys of sunshine and warmth, or at least they could when the persistent grayness of their peninsula permitted them to see that far. Sanitariums, hotels, and even private schools began to locate in Marin during the late 1870s and 1880s. San Rafael would have a near hundred-room hotel, a private college, a military academy. Down the railroad near The Junction (as it was now called) was a Presbyterian seminary, which was soon to be joined by an orphanage. In 1880 a pamphlet appeared in San Francisco entitled "The Mount Tamalpais Cemetery, rural burying place for San Francisco." All these were the harbingers of the boom that was certain to come.

The land around the Blithedale Hotel had itself remained almost entirely undeveloped through most of the 1880s because Samuel Throckmorton had failed in his attempt to do for it what Shafter had done for Point Reyes. Throckmorton, despite maneuvers which left some questions about his honesty, could never quite free the land from the legal and financial tangle in which William Richardson had left it. In 1887 the estate of Samuel Throckmorton sold the land at the base of Mount Tamalpais to pay off a $100,000 mortgage.

The leader of the group which acquired the land was Joseph G. Eastland, a man much like Peter Donahue. In fact, Eastland had learned business at the Donahue foundry. In an interview given in 1885, he explained with obvious relish how the foundry had turned the frequent San Francisco fires to its own advantage; iron scavenged from ruins at less than a penny a pound could be recast and sold for more than twenty cents a pound.

By 1887 Eastland had long since risen to prominence on his own. In Marin he was best known for his association not with Donahue but with the rival to Donahue's railroad, the North Pacific Coast. He had been the second president of that line, and now served on its board of directors. This was a fact of some importance, for to develop Mill Valley (a name of Eastland's choice) a closer connection had to be made to the main line of the North Pacific Coast. A long wagon ride over a dusty road, however quaint for a vacationer, would scarcely be acceptable to a commuter who would be making the trip every working day.

In 1890 The Tamalpais Land and Water Company paid the

North Pacific Coast Railroad $20,000 to build a spur connecting Mill Valley to the railroad line. Soon Eastland's land company had sold Eastland's spur to Eastland's railroad. And not long after the trains began regular trips along this spur, Eastland's town had been laid out, and an auction was held. On May 31, 1890, more than three thousand people arrived at Mill Valley. By the end of that afternoon, two hundred acres had been sold for $300,000. Although they had sold only a portion of their holdings, Eastland and his backers had more than doubled their investment. (Even those who spoke up at the beginning of the auction could more than double their money; a lot sold early in the auction for $750 was re-sold a few months later for $1,650.)

In 1893 a visitor to the town of Eastland—Mill Valley in gratitude to its founder had changed its name the year before—was awed by what a boom could do in so short a time. "What was three years ago nothing but a stock ranch with not a sign of inhabitants is now one of the most beautiful locations in the state, with over 500 residents and a tourist population of 2,000. Fine residences have been built. The station is located in a group of redwoods and round about are scattered the business houses of the valley. They include two livery stables, two general stores, two butcher shops, and four hotels. The Hotel Bellevue and Hotel Eastland was within five minutes walk of the depot. There is an Episcopalian and a Catholic Church and an attractive schoolhouse....Over thirty miles of good wagon roads have been constructed, which are kept well watered; miles of sewers were built, and seven miles of water mains bring the purest mountain water down from the slopes of Tamalpais."

To read this account of the town of Eastland, and to read the *Souvenir* published that same year of 1893, would make the boom of the Marin Peninsula seem assured. But this was far from the case. Indeed, the 1893 *Souvenir* might well have been an attempt by the economic leaders of Marin to breathe new life into a movement that was already beginning to falter.

In 1893 the economy of California was in a severe depression. Busts, not booms, were the order of the day. The pressures of this trying time were apparently too much even for Joseph Eastland himself; he died of cerebral hemmorrhage in 1895. The population of Marin, which had grown from 6,903 to 11,324 in the 1880s, almost stood still in the 1890s; the census of 1900 recorded it as 13,072. Moreover, land values were on the decline. As one Marin newspaper reported in 1895: "If the plain truth be told, the county, notwithstanding its magnificent natural advantages, has been on the downgrade. There is very little tillable land that will bring today within twenty five per cent of the price it commanded five years back."

What to the proponents of "improvement" looked like stagnation was not entirely due to the general state of the California economy. Part of it was due to the way Marin itself had developed. And the very proximity to San Francisco which made Marin seem so suitable for suburban development had now at the same time revealed disadvantages.

The railroads in their attempt to increase profits had advertised heavily in San Francisco the advantages of a weekend in Marin. And this advertising had been successful. There were more trains and ferries to Marin on the weekends to serve visitors than there were during the week to serve residents. Thus, each weekend the trains distributed throughout Marin precisely those very urban low-lifes from whom Marin commuters had hoped to preserve their families.

"Sunday last was a lovely day in San Rafael. The beauty of springtime brought thousands of San Francisco people who enjoyed our town and its environs. On the other hand, the day was one of the most disgraceful ever experienced in our town. A great number of vile characters swarmed in the streets and country roads and displayed their vileness in various acts of vulgarity and violence.... Companies of drunken men and women despoiled yards and gardens and insulted citizens outrageously."

This the Marin *Journal* reported after one weekend, and such reports became a staple of the Monday issues. Sausalito, now a town of 2,400 due to the ferry terminal, was reputed to be the center of Bay Area vice. It was a town said to be run by "the pool room lobby"; and drunkenness and foul language were not the worst of its public vices. (Sausalito's most distinguished citizen was the journalist William Randolph Hearst, who lived there openly with his mistress.) Once, when the county sheriff attempted to crack down on the gambling, he found himself being arrested by the Sausalito police for disturbing the peace.

As early as 1890 this problem was obvious enough that Joseph Eastland had written a prohibition of the sale of liquor into the land titles for his town. By 1900, the local merchants insisted that the town of Eastland be incorporated for the sake of public order. And Eastland was fairing better than elsewhere. The Junction was now noted not only for its Presbyterians, but also for its saloons, affectionately called "blind pigs."

Eastland, however, even after incorporation was scarcely a town. Most, perhaps four out of five, of the houses built after the auction were country homes that were occupied only on weekends and for a month or two during the summer. The town was really no more than the old Blithedale Hotel spread out over two hundred acres. It would only "boom" into existence once its economy was built on permanent residents, not upon the tourists.

One expression of the town's frustration may well have been its decision in 1904 to change its name back to Mill Valley. The town was choking on its own early growth; Eastland himself must have been somehow responsible. Of course, no individual was responsible and neither was any individual responsible for the event of 1906 which began the boom predicted in 1893, a boom which continues to the present day.

The great earthquake of 1906 was centered in western Marin, near Tomales Point. The bayside of Marin was largely spared from the effects, as if Mount Tamalpais protected it from both fogs and earthquakes. San Francisco was not spared, and a subsequent fire burned out of control until much of the city was ashes and ruins. This destruction of San Francisco was the making of Marin County.

Thousands of San Franciscans who had lost their homes moved permanently to the summer homes of Marin. Once again, new towns seemed to be springing spontaneously from the soil. Less than a year after the great San Francisco fire, a town was incorporated around the Junction. (This town, in honor of its seminary, took the name of a British theologian—albeit in Spanish spelling; and San Anselmo, British scholastic in Spanish garb, would soon cast out the blind pigs.)

Within another year, two more towns had been incorporated along the railway between the Junction and the Mill Valley spur. Mill Valley itself had been transformed into a town of more than 2,500 permanent inhabitants. Even naughty Sausalito, although never entirely respectable, began to take steps in that general direction; by 1909 a reform ticket had been elected to city office, and the last of the notorious poolhalls had been closed. The next year the census would show that Marin's population had almost doubled between 1900 and 1910, almost all of that growth coming in the four years after the destruction of San Francisco.

The independent railroads which had made the development of the Marin Peninsula possible were themselves doomed by 1906. The North Pacific Coast had been virtually ruined by the depression of 1893. When Oscar Shafter's brother died that very year, he was found to be almost bankrupt. *A Report of the Marin County Ranches of James McM. Shafter, Deceased*, published the same year, signaled the beginning of the dissolution of the small empire Oscar Shafter had spent much of his maturity consolidating. Those who now bought portions of it would find their titles clear beyond question.

The North Pacific Coast and Donahue's railroad scarcely survived to see the boom they had helped make possible. The year after the San Francisco fire they were merged, and taken over by the transcontinental giants, the Southern Pacific and the Santa Fe. Nonetheless, independent railroading was then still enjoying one small, final triumph on the Marin Peninsula.

The North Pacific Coast Railroad had broken the spine of the peninsula, but only at a weak point, White's Hill. In 1896, it had been decided that another railroad was to assault the ridge at its strength. A track would run from Mill Valley up Mount Tamalpais itself; the mountain would be used for a pleasure ride, a tourist attraction.

The originators of this plan were mostly businessmen or large landholders in the area around Mill Valley who were concerned about the faltering economy. Sidney Cushing, for instance, the president of the newly formed corporation, was owner of the Blithedale Hotel which had been founded by his father. The Mill Valley & Mount Tamalpais Railway, even if only modestly successful, would increase the value of such a local business many times over.

The depression in one way helped them. They could engage a construction company which was so eager for work that it took payment largely in stock. The construction company, in turn, could take more out of the bones and sinews of their workers than was even customary for a Donahue or Eastland. At the beginning of construction, the workers were being paid approximately ten dollars for a sixty-hour week. Moreover, the men were forced to live in a company camp, and to eat at the company canteen, all of which was deducted from their pay. As a result, after sixty hours of work a man was left with at most a dollar to take home to his family.

Some who could not stand the conditions and left before a full week found that their net wages were not enough to pay for the ferry back to San Francisco.

In February, 1896, there was, understandably, a threat of a strike. The construction head was not worried; anyone who did not like the conditions or wages could quit: "There are plenty ready and willing to take their places." Rumors spread among the predominantly Irish workers that the company was planning to replace them all with Chinese and Italians willing to work for a dollar a day. Finally, Sidney Cushing himself arrived to settle the dispute. He found that the chief difficulty lay with the cook, who happened to be Chinese; never again would Irish workers be asked to eat half-cooked potatoes. With that concession made, work resumed as usual.

The next month there was another crisis, this one more dangerous. In order to connect their scenic railroad with the main line, the directors of the new railroad had decided to make use of one of the two main streets of Mill Valley. Moreover, they decided to run their rails down the center of this street, making it virtually useless for other traffic.

The ordinary residents of Mill Valley, who were already sensitive about the influx of tourists of questionable character, quickly formed an association to take the railroad to court. A temporary injunction was gained by this group against further construction in Mill Valley. When during the trial the railroad clearly violated this injunction by distributing building materials along the disputed route, able Sidney Cushing convinced the judge, over the protests of the property owners, that this distribution had been the innocent mistake of workmen ignorant of the area.

When the judge subsequently found in favor of the railroad, the property owners might have thought they had only lost the first round of what was going to be a long fight. But then they learned why the innocent mistake had been made. The temporary injunction was lifted late in the afternoon, too late for any further legal maneuvering. By the next morning, all the track had been laid through Mill Valley. Using the materials that had already been distributed, the laborers had worked into the night, by the light of bonfires, and had been rewarded with an extra half-day's pay.

Now no human obstacles remained for the Mount Tamalpais Railroad, and the natural ones seems tractable. The railway had only to twist and turn as it moved up to the summit. "The crookedest railroad in the world," as it came to be called, was open to the public in August, 1896.

The railroad flourished. Its locomotives—the largest of which would be called "The Joseph G. Eastland"—had carried 23,000 passengers by the end of the very first year. It became almost a necessary excursion for any tourist visiting San Francisco; on Mount Tamalpais one could see the bay region as a whole. Travel writers outdid themselves in praise of the railroad—"the most charming and unique of Califiornia's gifts to the World," one wrote.

By 1904, two taverns had been built near the summits of Mount Tamalpais. A gravity car trip down to a particularly impressive stand of redwoods in a nearby canyon—"the longest rollercoaster ride in the world"—was added soon after. By 1911, the railroad had become so profitable that there was even talk of extending it across the ridge to Bolinas; but, like all the plans to bring the once thriving lumber port into the "boom" of Marin County, this one came to nothing.

For one decade, and then a second, the railroad thrived. But the mountain had not been entirely conquered. The operators of the railroad had a scare in 1913 when the far slope of Tamalpais burned; 7,000 men fought that fire and preserved both the railroad and the taverns. When tourists now looked out to the sea, they would have to gaze over a blackened landscape. More importantly, this fire was not an unusual incident in the long history of the mountain; the flora with which it was covered made that certain.

This mountain flora was unlike any that predominated on either the ocean or baysides of the Marin Peninsula. The ocean side of Marin, cooled by the summer fogs, was covered with conifer forests that seem to have stretched into California from far to the north; in contrast, the bayside, protected from the same fogs and hence having hot, dry summers, was largely oak-studded grasslands that seem to have stretched into California from the south. In certain places the oceanside-bayside contrast can be even more striking. In the coolest, moistest canyons of Marin can occasionally be found a variety of fern whose typical locale is the Aleutian Islands; in the hottest, driest canyons, only a few miles away, can be found a small blackish fern which also survives in the Sonoran desert.

Mount Tamalpais and its ridge separate these two contrasting floras, and it is covered with a flora of its own, a flora peculiar to California, the chaparral. The chaparral is not a group of plants about which travel literature or investment brochures have much to say. It is an unattractive combination of shrubs, stunted trees, and related plants. It offers man neither lumber for his use nor pasture for his herds. (Some of the shrubs, such as greasewood, even secrete poison into the soil to prevent herbaceous growth.) Nor does the chaparral offer the dignity of the forest or the vistas of a grassland. To try to travel through it is to be continually pricked and scratched, and to risk losing one's bearings in its midst. The Indians could find their way only by following paths broken by bears, and they also shared the bears' taste for the berries produced by some of the shrubs. Nonetheless, when they sought to explain mythically why they themselves were passing away in the face of the whiteman, they said simply that they had been fashioned not from the wood of the conifer or the oak but from the wood of the chaparral, a wood hollow and weak.

One American botanist lamely attempted to make the chaparral picturesque by describing it as an "elfin forest." Elfin it is, but most notably in its capacity for making mischief for those who try to live near it. During the dry California summers the chaparral is perfect kindling. And this flammability is in its own interest, for after a few years it tends to become choked on its own growth. But after a fire it comes back vigorously; it thrives on periodic razing. And, it is through flames that the other two floras find their differences resolved on the separating ridge of Tamalpais. To survive, these other plants had to adapt to the frequent fires that sweep out of the chaparral. One group of pines, peculiar to California, no longer drops its cones except with a fire, the seedlings then coming to life in the ashes of their parents. Some herbaceous plants peculiar to the chaparral are only seen after a major fire; one such plant, an exquisitely cream-colored lily—the so-called fire lily—will live for a few weeks after a fire, then drop its seeds which will then wait years, perhaps even decades, for the bloom of the next great fire.

The Mill Valley & Mount Tamalpais Railway twisted and turned its way to the top of Mount Tamalpais mostly through chaparral. Hundreds of thousands of passengers took this trip, and the railway flourished, while the elves became stifled in their own growth and waited for renewal. Then in 1920 part of the Mountain bloomed; one of the taverns was destroyed, and much of the railroad track had to be relaid. And then on July 2, 1929, the whole mountain bloomed. The railway was swept away, never to return;

and for a time Mill Valley itself seemed doomed as the fire moved up Blithedale Canyon destroying more than one hundred homes.

Many stories were told of that great fire. The unfortunate guests at the tavern were only saved by a heroic engineer who drove the train back down through the flames. It was said that he had his eyebrows singed off, and that his frightened passengers only preserved themselves from the heat and smoke by covering their faces with blankets liberally soaked with the tavern's best champagne.

The story was also told of two women, best friends, standing together in safety, watching from a distance as the flames progressed up the canyon toward the house of one. When the fire finally reached the house, it was engulfed so completely, so instanteously, and the fire itself from that distance was so lovely, that the friend of the woman whose house was destroyed could not help but gasp what a spectacular sight its burning made. The other never spoke to her again.

Soon after this great fire in which the railroad was destroyed and the town saved only through the caprice of the wind, the lilies burst forth from the mountain in profusion, magnificent inflorescences of cream, some taller than a man.

Between the first permanent European settlement on Marin and the boom of 1906 less than a century had passed. An infant baptized on the first day of the mission would have been less than sixty years old when railroad men celebrated with champagne the conquering of White's Hill. The introduction of agriculture, the establishment of ranches, the growth of small towns—it had all happened in less than a century. Indian. Franciscan. Mexican. Yankee. A hundred years before the fire of 1929 Juan Amoros was still serving his God in San Rafael.

The peninsula had been civilized; it now had a recorded history, as it had not when Serra looked across at it in 1775. Machines now dominated the peninsula. Its natural skeleton had been supplanted by an artificial one of rails, rails which wound up hills, trestled over marshes and occasionally burrowed through ridges. The railways had made the "boom" of Marin possible, and no sooner had this boom begun in 1906 than the locomotives themselves were being supplanted by automobiles and would eventually disappear from the Marin Peninsula altogether.

By the early twentieth century, the peninsula had become

ringed with institutions of protection. There were the lighthouses that had so impressed Richard Henry Dana; these protected navigation. There were military installations; the southern tip of Marin was now a series of gun implantments and other fortifications that were to preserve the bay region from invasion. Angel Island itself was not only fortified but also had become an immigration station to process those who wished to enter the country legally. And from Angel Island one could see the prison that had been built at San Quentin for unruly elements within California, the prison itself being there as the result of a land speculator's last desperate attempt at solvency. The newest of these institutions were the parks that strove to protect what was left of the indigenous life of Marin from the forces which had supplanted the rest; the redwood canyon, to which the Mount Tamalpais Railroad sent its "gravity cars," was saved from being flooded by a reservoir only through being ceded to the United States Government—only by government action could such places be preserved. Lighthouses to protect men from nature, prisons and guns to protect men from each other, even parks to protect nature from men—so much had changed from the time, only two lifetimes before, when grizzlies ruled the peninsula and the Indians respected them, and wondered at them, and at the coyotes, and also at the whales and galleons in their annual migrations.

But perhaps even these Indians sometimes dreamt of dominance over the nature that gave them succor. It was reported of a tribe just to the north of Marin that the mere possession of a grizzly pelt could drive a man mad. Such a "human grizzly," as he was called, would think himself one with the grizzly, possessor of its powers and license. He would have to be secretive about his transformation, for if his fellow villagers knew of it they would surely kill him. But when the occasion arose, he would slip away from his village, recite the proper incantations, don his pelt with his head beneath its fangs and his hands in its claws, and then hunt human beings as he thought the grizzly did, to sup off them.

The grizzly bear is now gone, and today no one can be certain if "human grizzlies" ever really existed outside the imagination of those who feared them. Nature itself has long since become an object of domination, and also of sentimental attachment, much as the Mexican ranchers in their last days told sentimental stories about Indian braves.

On the Marin Peninsula, a culmination of this dominance of nature was reached a few years after the Mount Tamalpais Railway was abandoned, when it was decided to end the separate existence of the Marin Peninsula by bridging it to the rebuilt peninsula of San Francisco. To fulfill this vision of its destiny, Marin had to cease to be a peninsula at all. Marin was to end its peninsular existence in order to become part of a larger isthmus.

This feat of engineering, it was maintained, was not being performed simply for human convenience, however much the bridge would facilitate the transport of goods and people. It was also to be a bridge to the mainstream of human history, a mainstream governed by impersonal forces at once rational and benign. Such at least was the optimistic philosophy that some invoked to promote the project.

"From the first caveman who, uneasily, made comradeship with an equally suspicious fellow man, to the last court of nations seeking hopefully the end of war and conquest, all of the hidden and mysterious forces of the world have steadily worked for the closer communion of men, for their ultimate union in one vast brotherhood."

When George Sterling wrote these words in 1925, he expected his fellow Californians who lived about San Francisco Bay to accept their truth as self-evident. It was made self-evident by the transformation of the bay area region through the contact of European civilization, a transformation they had witnessed.

The Golden Gate was no gateway when men first came to know it. Rather, it was a barrier which inhibited human contact. The Golden Gate and San Francisco Bay had contributed to the fragmentation of the original Californians into small tribal groups which did not even share a common tongue. And the mother sea itself had for centuries reinforced this fragmentation by isolating these tribes from the integrating genius of European civilization.

The Europeans eventually gained a fragile mastery over the mindless vicissitudes of the sea. And eventually they came into San Francisco Bay. And the Golden Gate which for tens of centuries had contributed to the frustration of man's higher impulses became suddenly transformed into an instrument of their realization. The strait was now truly a gateway, a golden gateway through which men would come who had the means to overcome tribal differences, to effect closer communions.

This at least was how the past looked from Sterling's vantage, a vantage he believed his fellow Californians would share; and once they thus saw the past, then the forces governing human history were no longer so hidden, so mysterious. Sterling and his fellow Californians could see these universal forces as they had been at work in the microcosm of this one geographical region. If such forces were manifest anywhere, they were manifest in a region such as this one, a region which had progressed so greatly, so quickly.

To the existence of these forces Sterling wished more than merely philosophical assent. These were forces not just of the past, but of all historical time. To perceive their operation in the past is to become aware of the duty to cooperate with them in the present and the future. Sterling, for one, thought he knew what these forces required next—or rather what they required of that small portion of mankind that lived around San Francisco Bay.

The Golden Gate, however much it now assisted commerce with the larger world, still inhibited contact between the persons who lived to the south of the bay and those who lived to its north. Most immediately, it was a physical barrier between San Francisco and Marin. There must be a closer communion between the people of the region. And physical connection was a necessary condition for this closer communion.

The Golden Gate must be bridged; the two peninsulas must become a single isthmus. A Golden Gate Bridge would stand as witness to "a faith in man that is within us, and to our devotion to that faith." It would, it *will* stand as an assurance that "the race of man shall endure into the ages."

It was fitting that George Sterling should have given the most elevated justification for the bridge. He himself was widely regarded as the greatest poet that California had yet produced. He alone of living writers had had his words carved into a triumphal arch at the San Francisco Panama-Pacific Exposition of 1915-16; there they were given equal place with those of Dante, Cervantes, Shakespeare, Goethe. This was to signify, as was the Exposition as a whole, that California had entered the mainstream of world history. The Exposition was a celebration of this fact; the Golden Gate Bridge would be its permanent monument.

When the completion of this bridge was celebrated eleven years later (by which time Sterling's own reputation as a great poet was already a thing of the past and he himself long dead by his own hand), this essay, "The Bridge of Ages," still so well expressed the professed ideals of the builders that it was given a featured place in the official program.

And perhaps history really does look like this to those who think they see in its whirling forces the elements of an empire for themselves. Perhaps history as a whole does look like the progressive building of a bridge.

But it will not look like this to anyone who, rather than seeking empire, simply attends to the detailed history of a small and unimportant place, like the Marin Peninsula. To see the forces of history acting here is to see them acting on a human scale. Here, human faces are not lost in the shadows of monumental inevitabilities. Here, those displaced in the name of higher communions can still be heard before their leaving, heard more clearly than they can amidst the noise of a larger place.

From such a perspective history looks less like the progressive building of a bridge than it does like the irregular growth of the chaparral, a growth renewed only through general conflagrations to human eyes at once horrifying and beautiful.

Epilogue

On the broken shore now called the Marin Peninsula has been acted out the glory and folly of the human experience; here, as elsewhere under the sun, has been revealed the vanity of human wishes. It has been the stage and setting for the rise and fall of empires, whether that "empire" be the dream of one man, the gains of one group, or the course of a nation. The aboriginal village, the Spanish mission, the Mexican ranch, the American small town—each was here, each changing the land and changed by it, each considering itself the stable, secure end of historical development, and each in turn swept away, all finally historical spindrift. "One generation passeth away and another generation cometh: but the earth abideth forever."

Where are we to seek the resolution of human history? How can its changes seem to us at once both beautiful and horrifying? Can this paradox be resolved? Some might look to nature for resolution, to the earth which abideth forever. Perhaps there things are at peace, and will reveal it if only we can find the right question to ask. Perhaps.

The Marin landscape itself suggests a question to ask of it. It is a place broken, set against itself as if reflecting this paradox of human history; it is two peninsulas, strangely juxtaposed, apparently at cross-purposes. How did the Marin Peninsula and Point Reyes ever become parts of the same place? The geologists of today think they know, and the story they tell involves the whole earth—and even then says more than they intend, for it shares in part the shape of a myth.

The earth, they say, has a molten core, on which all the land we know—whole continents, even the bedrock of the ocean floor—floats like gigantic congealed crusts. Only the volcano gives us a

167

glimpse of the fire-blood of our world. Once, a very long time ago, long before man, all the dry crusts we call continents were one. This land geologists call Pangaea. Why this original, unified land did not endure no one knows. Suffice it to say, Pangaea began to fall apart. Large pieces broke off, and drifted away. One of these was the continent we now call North America. North America drifted toward the ocean of water we now call the Pacific. But the bedrock of the Pacific floor, no less than that of North America, was merely a crust formed out of, and drifting upon, the molten sea at the heart of our world. And the eastern shelf of the Pacific floor was moving toward North America, toward an inevitable collision.

When the collision occurred, at first neither recoiled. The towering continent simply rode over the edge of the Pacific floor plunging it into the sea of fire. This was a collision on a titanic scale; it ended not in a decade, or a century, or a millenium. It has not ended yet. It began before all life existed, and might still be continuing long after life on this planet is spent. Or so our geologists tell us.

So long has this collision continued, so long did the Pacific floor continue to move toward North America even after it had begun to be turned toward the depths, that the fragments of ocean rock scraped off on the western side of North America became compressed into a distinctive formation of considerable size. Thus rocks originally formed thousands of miles apart on the ocean floor are now to be found on the Pacific coast, jumbled together in that geological nightmare called the Franciscan.

Some of the bedrock sent into the depths, plunged into the ocean of fire, had a fate more extraordinary still. Softened, purified, transmuted, it somehow forced its way back up through the cracked crust of North America, more than a hundred miles from the coast. There it crystallized into granite megaliths which erosion of the earth above eventually revealed in their naked glory, the dark and deathlike wall of the Sierra Nevada.

The collision began long before life existed and will perhaps continue long after life itself is a thing of the past; nonetheless, the end of the collision is in sight, at least for those who view change through geological eyes. For centuries now, the Pacific floor has already begun to recoil from the continent, to deflect toward the northwest. And it has been dragging with it the southernmost portion of the Sierra Nevada granite, by which it had become attached to the continent. This is how there came to be juxtaposed to the Marin Peninsula that coyote head of granite, Point Reyes—it is the remains of a southern Sierra Nevada mountain which has been dragged hundreds of miles by the Pacific floor in its retreat.

Now we can begin to see the mythic shape that looms behind this geological story, the myth of a fortunate fall. A lost brother, having triumphed over adversity, returns in glory to protect the defeated one he left behind. The noble Point Reyes, reunited with the humbled Franciscan, now protects him against the worst ravages of the sea. The story could end here if it really were a myth told by men for the sake of other men. But this story, if true, is a story told by nature for the sake of no one. Thus the story still continues, longer than it should. The protection of Point Reyes will not abide.

The sea floor with its granite is still moving away from the coast. It moves a few inches a year, although that movement is far from uniform. Frequently, the Pacific and North American titans are locked together somewhere along their surface of contact, as if North America had for a time caught the Pacific in its flight. But nothing can stop the movement for long, at least by geological measure. The pressure gradually builds on the locked land until the resistance is crushed, and the titans temporarily spring free. At that moment the land on each side suddenly lurches, a few inches, a foot, perhaps ten. The land lurches groaning and shuddering, the very earth seems to quake.

And so the story continues even to this day. Point Reyes will not remain next to Marin forever. It is being moved, moved by forces of inhuman might, away from the continent, back to the sea, where one day it will be an island, or an anomalous bank, or perhaps nothing noticeable at all. Marin is geologically a temporary thing, in the process of being rent.

Between Point Reyes and the Marin Peninsula proper there already exists a depression in the land, the southern half a valley, the northern a finger-shaped bay. This depression bears witness that whatever attempts to bridge these contrary peninsulas will eventually be rendered unto dust.

The coyote waits for its freedom, for the return of its head to the open sea.

The Hub in San Anselmo
Courtesy of Marin County Historical Society

The Marin County Courthouse in downtown San Rafael, 1872–1971
Courtesy Marin County Historical Society

Sources

The sources used in the writing of each section are organized alphabetically. When there has seemed to me to be an obvious division in the materials used for a section, I have divided my bibliography accordingly. For instance, the reader will find the sources for Chapter 1, Section 2, divided into two parts, one works on the name "California," the other on Cortes.

Abbreviations

AHR: *American Historical Review.*

Ba: Bancroft Library, University of California at Berkeley.

BW: Hubert H. Bancroft, *Works* (San Francisco, 1883-91).

CHSQ: *California Historical Society Quarterly.*

HAC: Warren A. Beck and Ynez D. Haase, *Historical Atlas of California* (Norman, 1974).

IJ: San Rafael *Independent Journal.*

MHi: Marin Historical Society, San Rafael, California.

OM: *Old Marin with Love* (San Rafael, 1975).

PHR: *Pacific Historical Review.*

SCQ: *Southern California Quarterly* (Before 1962 called *Historical Society of Southern California Quarterly*).

Epigraphs

Robinson Jeffers, *The Selected Poetry* (New York, 1951); Czeslaw Milosz, *Selected Poems* (New York, 1973).

171

Prologue; Epilogue

David Alt, *Roadside Geology of Northern California* (Missoula, 1975); T. Atwater, "Implications of Plate Tectonics for...Western North America," Geological Society of America *Bulletin* 81 (1970): 3513-36; E. H. Bailey, W. P. Irwin, and D. L. Jones, *Franciscan and Related Rocks* (San Francisco, 1964); Norman Hinds, *Evolution of the California Landscape* (San Francisco, 1963); Arthur D. Howard, *Evolution of the Landscape of the San Francisco Bay Region* (Berkeley, 1962); Robert Jacopi, *Earthquake Country* (Menlo Park, 1964); Olaf P. Jenkins, *Geologic Guide Book of the San Francisco Bay Counties* (San Francisco, 1962); Scientific American, *Continents Adrift* (San Francisco, 1972).

I. Nova Albion

Section 1

K. R. Andrews, "The Aims of Drake's Expedition of 1577-80," AHR v. 73 (1968), pp. 724-41; Robert F. Heizer, *Elizabethan California* (Ramona, Calif., 1974); J. S. Holliday, et al., "The Francis Drake Controversy," CHSQ v. 53 (1974), pp. 196-292; R. C. Temple, *The World Encompassed and Analogous Contemporary Documents* (London, 1926); George M. Thomson, *Sir Francis Drake* (London, 1972); H. R. Wagner, *Sir Francis Drake's Voyage Around the World* (San Francisco, 1926).

Section 2

Donald C. Cutter, "Sources of the Name 'California'," *Arizona and the West* v. 3 (1961), pp. 233-43; E. G. Gudde, "The Name 'California'," *Names* v. 2 (1954), pp. 121-33; Edward Everett Hale, *The Queen of California* (San Francisco, 1945); Ruth Putnam, "California, The Name," *University of California Publications in History* v. 4 (1917), pp. 293-365.

HAC, No. 1; W. Michael Mathes, *The Conquistador in California* (Los Angeles, 1973); Robert Miller, "Cortes and the First Attempt to Colonize California," CHSQ v. 53 (1974), pp. 5-16.

Section 3

Arthur Keller, Oliver Lissitzyn, and Frederick Mann, *Creation of Rights of Sovereignty Through Symbolic Acts 1400-1800* (New York, 1938); R. F. Heizer, *California's Oldest Historical Relic?* (Berkeley, 1972); Manual P. Servín, "Symbolic Acts of Sovereignty in Spanish California," SCQ v. 45 (1963), pp. 109-21; H. R. Wagner, *Juan Rodriquez Cabrillo* (San Francisco, 1941).

Sections 4 and 5

Raymond Aker, *The Cermenho Expedition at Drakes Bay* (Point Reyes, 1965); HAC, No. 12-3; R. F. Heizer, "Archaeological Evidence of Sebastian Rodriguez Cermeno's California Visit in 1595," CHSQ v.20 (1941), pp. 315-28; R. F. Heizer and C. W. Meighan, "Archaeological Exploration of 16th Century Indian Mounds at Drakes Bay," CHSQ v. 31 (1952), pp. 99-106; Maurice G. Holmes, *From New Spain by Sea to the Californias* (Glendale, 1963); W. M. Mathes, *Vizcaino and Spanish Expansion in the Pacific Ocean* (San Francisco, 1968); William Shurz, *The Manila Galleon* (New York, 1939); H. R. Wagner, "The Voyage to California of Sebastian Rodriguez Cermeno in 1595," CHSQ, v. 3 (1924), pp. 3-24; Henry R. Wagner, *Spanish Voyages to the Northwest Coast of California* (San Francisco, 1929).

II. The Island of the Angels
Sections 1 and 5

BW 18: 240-256; Herbert E. Bolton, *Outpost of Empire* (New York, 1931); Vincente Santa Maria, *The First Spanish Entry into San Francisco Bay, 1775* ed. by John Galvin (San Francisco, 1971); Theodore Treutlein, *San Francisco Bay: Discovery and Colonization, 1769-1776* (San Francisco, 1968).

Section 2

BW 18: 110-125; Herbert E. Bolton, "The Mission as a Frontier Institution in Spanish American Colonies," *Wider Horizons in American History* (New York, 1939); Charles E. Chapman, *The Founding of Spanish California* (New York, 1916); Peter Dunne, "The Expulsion of the Jesuits from New Spain," *Mid-America* v. 19 (1937), pp. 3-30; Zephyrin Engelhardt, *The Missions and Missionaries of California*, v. 2 (San Francisco, 1912), Part I; Maynard Geiger, "Instruction Concerning the Occupation of California, 1769," SCHQ v. 47 (1965), pp. 209-18; Herbert I. Priestley, *José de Galvez* (Berkeley, 1916).

Section 3

Lawrence Cunningham, *Saint Francis of Assisi* (Boston, 1976); Joan M. Erikson, *Saint Francis and his Four Ladies* (New York, 1970); Marion A. Habig (ed.), *St. Francis of Assisi: Writings and Early Biographies* (Chicago, 1973); John Moorman, *A History of the Franciscan Order from its Origins to the Year 1516* (Oxford, 1968); F. J. Polley, "The Original Father Junipero," *Historical Journal of*

Southern California v. 5 (1901), pp. 134-45; Paul Sabatier, *Life of St. Francis of Assisi,* tr. L. S. Houghton (New York, 1894).

BW 18: 126-182; Sibley Morrill, *The Texas Cannibals* (Oakland, 1964); Francisco Palou, *Life of Fray Junipero Serra,* trans. Maynard Geiger (Washington, 1955); Maynard J. Geiger, *The Life and Times of Fray Junipero Serra* (Washington, 1959).

Section 4

Academy of Pacific Coast History, *Publications,* vs. 1-2 (1910-1), passim; Fernand Bonev Companys, *Don Gaspar de Portola* (Serida, 1970); HAC, No. 15-17; Theodore E. Treutlein, "The Portola Expedition of 1769-70," CHSQ v. 47 (1968), pp. 291-314.

III. The Mission of Saint Raphael
Sections 1, 4, and 5

BW 19: 329-31, 450-539; Jacob N. Bowman, "The Resident Neophytes of the California Missions," SCQ 40(1958), pp. 138-48; Jacob N. Bowman and George W. Hendry, *The Spanish and Mexican Adobe and Other Buildings* (Ms., Ba), Part I, Section A; C. C. Colley, "The Missionization of the Coast Miwok Indians in California," CHSQ v. 49 (1970), pp. 143-62; Florence Donnelly, "Story of Mission San Rafael Archangel," IJ 10/14/67, 10/21/67; Engelhardt, *op. cit.,* v. 3 (San Francisco, 1913), pp. 31-183 passim; Maynard J. Geiger, *Franciscan Missionaries of Alta California, 1769-1848: A Biographical Dictionary* (San Marino, 1969), pp. 11-3, 104-6; John A. Hussey, *Mission San Rafael Arcangel* (Ms., Ba); Otto von Kotzebue, *A New Voyage round the World* (London, 1830), v. 2; *Libros de mision de San Rafael* (Ms., Ba); August M. Vaz, *The Northern Missions* (unpublished diss., Berkeley); Edith B. Webb, *Indian Life at the Old Missions* (Los Angeles, 1952).

Section 2

Robin Doughty, "The Farallones and the Boston Men," CHSQ v. 53 (1974), pp. 309-16; William A. Gale, "Albatross Log Book," in William D. Phelps, *Solid Men of Boston* (Ms., Ba); Frank A. Golden, *Russian Expansion on the Pacific, 1641-1850* (Gloucester, Mass., 1960); HAC Nos. 18, 40; August Mahr, *The Visit of the Rurik to San Francisco in 1816* (Stanford, 1932); Adele Ogden, *California Sea Otter Trade* (Berkeley, 1941); Francis J. Weber, "The California Missions and their Visitors," *The Americas* v. 24 (1968), pp. 319-36; Ynez Haase, *Russian American Company in California* (unpubl. diss., Berkeley).

Section 3

Geronimo Boscana, "Chinigchinich," in Alfred Robinson, *Life in California* (Santa Barbara, 1970); Sherburne F. Cook, *The Conflict between the California Indian and White Civilization* (Berkeley, 1976), Part I; Engelhardt, *op. cit.*, v.3; Maynard J. Geiger, *As the Padres Saw Them* (Glendale, 1976); C. Alan Hutchinson, "The Mexican Government and the Mission Indians of Upper California," *The Americas* v. 21 (1965), pp. 335-62; Francis J. Weber, *Documents of California's Catholic History* (Los Angeles, 1965); Francis J. Weber, "The Pious Fund of the Californias," *Hispanic American Historical Review* v. 43 (1963), pp. 78-94.

IV. Marin's Peninsula
Section 1

Engelhardt, *op. cit.*, v. 3: 581-91; Maynard J. Geiger, *Franciscan Missionaries*, pp. 200-3; Henry Peirce, *Memoranda of Past Events* (Ms., Ba); Peirce, *Rough Sketch* (Ms., Ba).

Section 2

BW 20: 301-62, 698-732; BW 21: 42-78; W. B. Campbell and J. R. Moriarity, "The Struggle over Secularization of the Missions on the Alta California Frontier," *Journal of San Diego History* v.15 (1963), pp. 3-16. Gerald J. Geary, *The Secularization of the California Missions* (Washington, 1934); Maynard J. Geiger, *Franciscan Missionaries*, pp. 158-60, 261-2; Woodrow J. Hansen, *The Search for Authority in California* (Oakland, 1960), chs. 21-5; Manual P. Servín, "The Secularization of the California Missions: a Reappraisal," SCQ 47 (1965); pp. 133-50.

Charles Brown, *Early Events* (Ms., Ba); Alice M. Cleaveland, *The North Bay Shore During the Spanish and Mexican Regimes* (unpbl. diss., Berkeley, 1957); Marion L. Lathrop, "The Indian Campaigns of General M. G. Vallejo," *Society of California Pioneers Quarterly* v. 9 (1932), pp. 161-205; Myrtle McKittrick, *Vallejo, Son of California* (Portland, Ore., 1944); Marcus Peterson, *The Career of Solano* (unpbl. diss., Berkeley, 1957); George Tays, "Mariano Guadelupe Vallejo and Sonoma—a biography and a history," CHSQ v.16 (1937), passim; Mariano Vallejo, *Historia de California* (Ms., Ba).

Section 3

J. P. Crevelli, *400 Years of Indian Affairs in the North Bay Counties* (unpbl. diss., Berkeley, 1959); Susanna Bryant Dakin, *The Lives of William Hartnell* (Stanford, 1949); Stephen Dietz, *Echa-*

Tamal (unpublished diss., San Francisco State); Jack Mason and Helen Van Cleave Park, *Early Marin* (Inverness, 1971), ch. 8; C. Hart Merriam, *Dawn of the World* (Cleveland, 1910), pp. 159-62; United States Land Cases 210ND, 392ND, 404ND (Ms., Ba).

Sections 4 and 5

Florence Donnelly, "The Story of Rancho Olompali," IJ 2/20/65; Edwin Gudde, *California Place Names* (Berkeley, 1969); Dorothy H. Huggins, "The Pursuit of an Indian Chief," *California Folklore Quarterly* v. 4 (1945) pp. 158-167; Lucretia Little, *Historical Documentation... to Restore and Preserve... Olompali* (San Rafael, 1973); Jack Mason, *op. cit.*, ch. 12; (J. Munro-Fraser), *History of Marin County* (San Francisco, 1880); Charles M. Slaymaker, *Cry for Olompali* (San Rafael, 1972); United States Land Grant Case 10ND (Ms., Ba).

V. Murphy's Day
Section 1
Joseph Revere, *Naval Duty in California* (Oakland, 1947).
Section 2
Florence Donnelly, "Charles A. Lauff—80 Years a Marinite," IJ 6/12/71; Donnelly, "The Don and his San Jose Rancho," IJ 10/7/67; Donnelly, "Marin's Irish Don," IJ 2/26/66; Donnelly, "The Reed Family Story," IJ 11/6/65; HAC, No. 29; Charles Lauff, 'Reminiscences," San Rafael *Independent* 1/25-5/23/16 (Ms, MHi); Jack Mason and Helen van Cleve Park, *op. cit.*, passim.

Faxon Dean Atherton, *California Diary*, ed. Doyce B. Nunis (San Francisco, 1964); Robert G. Cleland, *The Cattle on a Thousand Hills* (San Marino, 1951); Philip Edwards, *Diary* (San Francisco, 1932); William D. Phelps, *Fore and Aft* (Boston, 1871), chs. 21-29 Tracy Storer, *California Grizzly* (Berkeley, 1955).
Section 3
BW 34: passim; Robert H. Becker, *Diseños of California Ranchos* (San Francisco, 1964); Becker, *Designs on the Land* (San Francisco, 1969); Bowman and Hendry, *op. cit.*, Part I, Sections B and C; Eugene Duflot de Mofras, *Duflot de Mofras' Travels on the Pacific Coast*, trans. M.E. Wilbur (Santa Ana, 1937); Stephen Richardson, *The Days of the Dons* (Ms., Ba); W. W. Robinson, *Land in California* (Berkeley, 1948); Susan K. Tanner, *The Marin Peninsula: the Impact of Inhabitive Groups on the Landscape* (unpubl. diss., Berkeley, 1971), ch. 6; Henry Wise, *Los Gringos* (New York, 1849).

Section 4
Lee T. Burcham, *California Range Land* (Sacramento, 1957);
W. Clarke, *Vegetation Cover of San Francisco Bay Region in Early
Spanish Period* (unpbl. diss., Berkeley, 1959); Magdalen Coughlin,
"Boston Smugglers on the Coast: an Insight into the American Ac-
quisition of California," CHSQ 46 (1967): 99-120; Jesse E. Francis,
An Economic and Social History of Mexican California (unpbl. diss.,
Berkeley, 1935).

Section 5
Munro-Fraser, *op. cit.*, pp. 123-5.

VI. The Bear's Flag
Section 1
Florence Donnelly, "The Story of the Millers of Marin," IJ
7/10/71; Hugh Quigley, *Irish Race in California* (San Francisco,
1878), ch. 12; George R. Stewart, *The California Trail* (San Francisco, 1962); Stewart, *The Opening of the California Trail* (Berkeley,
1953).

Section 2
Charles L. Camp, "Kit Carson in California," CHSQ v.1 (1922),
pp. 111-51; Robert G. Cleland, "The Early Sentiment for the Annex-
ation of California," *Southwestern Historical Quarterly* v.18 (1914-5),
passim; Cleland, *This Reckless Breed of Men* (New York, 1952); HAC
42-4; John A. Hawgood, "The Pattern of Yankee Infiltration in Mexican Alta California," PHR 27 (1958): 27-38; Frederick Merk, *Manifest Destiny and Mission in American History* (New York, 1963);
The Monroe Doctrine and American Expansionism, 1843-49 (New
York, 1966); Dale L. Morgan, *Jedediah Smith* (Indianapolis, 1953).

Section 3
Bernard De Voto, *The Year of Decision, 1846* (Boston, 1942);
Ferol Egan, *Fremont* (Garden City, 1976); John C. Fremont, *Memoirs
of My Life* (Chicago, 1887); HAC, 46; Kenneth M. Johnson, *The
Fremont Court Martial* (Los Angeles, 1968); Josiah Royce, *California*
(Boston, 1886; Salt Lake City, 1971).

Francisco Arce, *Memorias Historicas* (Ms., Ba). Charles Brown,
Early Events (Ms., Ba); William Baldridge, *Days of 1846* (Ms., Ba);
Henry Fowler, *Dictation* (Ms., Ba); John Fowler, *Bear Flag Revolt*
(Ms., Ba); Archiebald Gillespie, "Gillespie and the Conquest of
California," CHSQ v.17 (1938), pp. 271-84; John Hawgood, "John
C. Fremont and the Bear Flag Revolution: a Reappraisal," SCQ v.49

(1962), pp. 67-96; John A. Hussey, *The United States and the Bear Flag Revolt* (unpbl. diss., Berkeley, 1941); Hussey, "New Light on the Original Bear Flag," CHSQ v. 31 (1952), pp. 205-15; Simeon Ide, *The Conquest of California* (Oakland, 1944); Werner H. Marti, *Messenger of Destiny* (San Francisco, 1960); Fred B. Rogers, "Bear Flag Lieutenant," CHSQ v. 29 (1950), pp. 266-78; Rogers, *William Brown Ide* (San Francisco, 1962); Rogers, "California Bear Flag of 1846," *California Blue Book* (Sacramento, 1958), pp. 9-12.

Section 4

John Dwyer, *One Hundred Years an Orphan* (Fresno, 1955); Florence Donnelly, "Capt. William Richardson: Sea Dog, Trader, Rancher," IJ 8/21/65; Joseph Ellison, *California and the Nation* (Berkeley, 1927), ch. 2; Boyd F. Huff, *El Puerto de los Balleneros* (Los Angeles, 1957); Paul W. Gates, "The Ajudication of Spanish-Mexican Land Claims in California," *Huntington Library Quarterly* v. 21 (1958), pp. 213-36; Gates, "The California Land Act of 1851," CHSQ 50 (1971): 395-430; Mason, *op. cit.*, ch. 3; Leonard Pitt, *The Decline of the Californios* (Berkeley, 1966), chs. 1-2; Stephen Richardson, *Days of the Dons* (Ms., Ba); William Richardson, *Salidas de Buques, 1837-8* (Ms., Ba); William T. Sherman, *Memoirs* (New York, 1875), v.1, pp. 68-9; Clyde F. Trudell, "Captain William Anthony Richardson," OM pp. 23-34; Helen Van Cleve Park, *Jose Yves Limantour* (Belvedere-Tiburon, 1966); Kenneth Johnson, *Jose Yves Limantour vs. the United States* (Los Angeles, 1961).

Section 5

Richard Henry Dana, *Two Years Before the Mast* (Boston, 1868; New York, 1936); Dana, *Journal*, ed. R. F. Lucid (Cambridge, Mass., 1968), pp. 843-925; D. H. Lawrence, *Studies in Classic American Literature* (New York, 1923), ch. 10; Kevin Starr, *Americans and the California Dream* (New York, 1973), pp. 38-47.

VII. Marin County
Section 1

Florence Donnelly, "The Story of Marin's Courthouse," IJ 2/5/66; Jack Mason and Helen Van Cleve Park, *The Making of Marin* (Inverness, Calif., 1975), ch. 2; Munro-Fraser, *op. cit.*; Marin *Journal*, 8/3/72; Helen Van Cleave Park and Clyde Trudell, "Old Courthouse History," OM, 173-9.

Section 2

Thomas Barfield and Jack Mason, *Last Stage for Bolinas* (Inverness, Calif., 1973), chs. 2-5; Owen C. Coy, *California County Boundaries* (Berkeley, 1923), pp. 158-60; Florence Donnelly, "Independent Journal Forerunner Four Page Weekly," IJ 8/28/71; Donnelly, "Marin Masons Mark Their 100th Birthday, 6/15/68; Donnelly, "Early Marin Justice," IJ 10/3/64; B.F. Gilbert, "The Confederate Minority in California," CHSQ v. 20 (1941), pp. 154-70; John Hussey, *Site of the Lighter Wharf* (Ms., Ba); T. Starr King, "Peace and What it would Cost Us," Marin County *Journal*, 9/17/ 1864; Jack Mason, *Point Reyes* (Inverness, Calif., 1972) Part II; Josiah Royce, *op. cit.*, chs. 3-4; Oscar Lovell Shafter, *Life, Diaries, and Letters* (San Francisco, 1915); Shafter, *Human Progress: Its Relation to Reason, Acting in Right Method* (Oakland, 1866); Edwin Sherman, *Fifty Years of Masonry in California* (San Francisco, 1898); Starr, *op. cit.*, 97-105; Susan Tanner, *op. cit.*, ch. 7.

Sections 3 and 4

Anon., *A Sketch of the Life of Peter Donahue* (San Francisco, 1885); A. Bray Dickinson, *Narrow Gauge to the Redwoods* (Los Angeles, 1967); Florence Donnelly, "William T. Coleman," IJ 9/28/68; Guy L. Dunscomb and Fred A. Stindt, *Northwestern Pacific Railroad* (Redwood City, 1964); Wallace W. Elliot, *San Rafael Illustrated* (San Francisco, 1884); Dorothy Gardiner, "Railroad's Role in Marin," IJ 8/28/71; Gilbert Kniess, *Redwood Railways* (Berkeley, 1956); James A. B. Scherer, *The Lion of the Vigilantes* (Indianapolis, 1939).

Dickinson, *op. cit.*, ch. 14; Joseph Eastland, *Dictation*(Ms., Ba.); Marin County Journal, *Souvenir of Marin County* (San Rafael, 1893); Mason and Park, *op. cit.*, ch. 4; Mill Valley Oral History Project, *Interviews* (Ms., Ba.); Mill Valley Record, *60th Anniversary of Mill Valley* (Mill Valley, 1960); Tanner, *op. cit.*, ch.8;

Section 5

Frederick Bowlen, *Their Hills Afire: The Story of the Mill Valley Conflagration, July 2, 1929* (Ms., California Historical Society San Francisco); Alvin Graves and Theodore Wurm, *The Crookedest Railroad in the World* (Fresno, 1954); Mason and Park, *op. cit.*, ch. 7; Mill Valley and Mount Tamalpais Railway, *Records* (Ms., Ba.); Mill Valley Oral History Project, *op. cit.*

D. I. Axelrod, "Evolution of the Madro-Tertiary Geoflora," *Botanical Review* 24 (1958): 433-509; Elna Bakker, *An Island Called California* (Berkeley, 1972), chs. 4-7; Alice Eastwood, *A Collection of Popular Articles on the Flora of Mount Tamalpais* (San Francisco,

1944); Francis Fultz, *The Elfin Forest* (Los Angeles, 1923); John Howell, *Marin Flora* (Berkeley, 1970); J.K. McPherson & C.H. Muller, "Allelopathic Effects of...Chamis" *Ecological Monographs,* 39 (1969): 177-98; Robert Ornduff, *Introduction to California Plant Life* (Berkeley, 1974), chs. 5, 7; J. R. Sweeney, "Responses of Vegetation to Fire," *University of California Publications in Botany* v. 28 (1956): pp. 143-250.

S. A. Barrett, "Pomo Bear Doctors," *University of California Publications in American Archeology and Ethnology* v.12 (1917), 443-67; Allen Brown, *Golden Gate* (Garden City, 1965); Porter Garnett, *The Inscriptions at the Panama-Pacific International Exposition* (San Francisco, 1915); Julia S. Hamilton, *Report of the Marin County Ranches of James McM. Shafter* (San Francisco, 1893); Tom Killion, *Fortress Marin* (San Rafael, 1979); Starr, *op. cit.,* pp. 267-85; George Sterling, "Bridge of Ages," in *Official Souvenir Programme: Golden Gate Bridge Fiesta* (San Francisco, 1937); Sterling, *Ode on the Opening of the Panama-Pacific International Exposition* (San Francisco, 1915); Sterling, *Robinson Jeffers* (New York, 1926).

Index